WHAT CHURCH LEADERS ARE SAYING ABOUT
Transition Apparitions

Intrigued by the proposition that interim ministry is "overdue for some rethinking," Russ began poking around in the Holy Cow! Consulting database and then turned (as he always does) to careful, systematic analysis of the data. He began rethinking his own thinking about pastoral transitions and came away absolutely convinced, as he said to me, "we need a new model." So he designed it.

Dr. James Pence, PhD, Walkalong Consulting

Pastoral transitions are critical periods in the life of congregations. Over the years, a body of assumed knowledge has grown up about the ways congregations react to the departure of a pastor and the solutions required to help deal with the ensuing emotions. These assumptions tend to result in one-size-fits-all approaches that ignore the fact that no two congregations are the same. They also lead to misinterpretations of what a congregation is actually experiencing during the transition period.

In this insightful book, Russell Crabtree presents an evidence-based case that debunks the traditional thinking around pastoral transition. Drawing upon an extensive database of case studies, Crabtree dismantles the ghosts inhabiting the long-established paradigm of pastoral transition and presents a new evidence-based model for succession planning. This book is must reading for regional association leaders, church consultants, church board members, and anyone who cares about the health and vitality of congregations.

Barry Frey, CTC, Business Consulting Team Leader,
Samaritan Business Consulting

This book beautifully articulates what astute consultants have noted for years. Fear of the unknown and its uncertainty is a basic human characteristic that is the source of poor decisions— then wandering in the desert, and finally feelings of resignation. For those who have faced that fear, it has too many times been replaced by discouragement. It stands to reason that if uncertainty is present throughout the system, the entire system will benefit from involvement in the transition process. Russ's book provides an empirical tool to prepare transition ministers to do this and do it well.

Dr. Keli Rugenstein, PhD, LCSW, LMFT, Staff Psychotherapist,
Director of Clergy and Congregation Care

I found this book illuminating. Russ's database of congregational assessments has allowed him to glimpse the unfiltered identity and needs of churches. Too often we think we know what is going on or needed in a congregation, but our assessments are built on assumptions and preconceived notions, not actual congregational feedback. Using the congregational feedback helps us understand that so many of our assumptions are simply unfounded.

At the same time this book doesn't offer us a simplistic view of the "average" congregation. Russ clearly illustrates the need for congregational assessment to understand the unique needs of each congregation.

After reading this text I came away not with a simple understanding of what was needed in pastors who would lead these congregations in transition, but with a realization that skills needed to help congregations in transition vary depending on the dynamics of the individual congregation.

Dr. James Fenimore, PhD, Congregational Consultant,
Samaritan Counseling Center

Heated conversations about interim ministry abound in judiciaries and congregations. This ministry model is decades old and requires an examination of assumptions in today's world of church.

There is palpable discontent across judiciaries, congregations, and clergy that centers on the goal of the interim time. In the past, the goal focused on congregations preparing to change pastors. Today, the goal is focused on culture change in congregations. This major shift demands new thinking about the role of the interim time and the preparation of interim ministers. It demands a new understanding of the dynamics of the interim time and a new set of assumptions around how best to engage a congregation in moving toward greater health and vitality.

Culture change is work that requires defined clergy skill sets based on a through and deep understanding of the church organization and culture. Russ Crabtree's use of organizational intelligence data provides a research-based gift to enlighten this ongoing conversation and to renew the model for this important ministry.

The results of Russ's study are compelling. They will invite you to shift your thinking about the interim time in congregations. This research has the potential to bring renewed value to the interim model and renewed life to congregations in transition—and will challenge creativity and breath new life into a decades old model of ministry.

Susan Czolgosz, Samaritan Interfaith Center

Transition Apparitions

TRANSITION APPARITIONS

Why Much of What We Know about Pastoral Transitions Is Wrong

J. RUSSELL CRABTREE

TRANSITION APPARITIONS
Why Much of What We Know about Pastoral Transitions Is Wrong

PUBLISHING CONSULTANT: Huff Publishing Associates, LLC
COVER IMAGE © Yupiramos Group | Dreamstime.com
ILLUSTRATIONS: page 87 © Jjesadaphorn | Dreamstime.com; page 89 © Robert Adrian Hillman | Dreamstime.com
COVER AND INTERIOR DESIGN: Marti Naughton

 PUBLISHED BY Magi Press
ISBN 978-0-692-49470-7

Acknowledgements

In the acknowledgements for *Owl Sight,* I indicated that the book had roughly 50,000 contributors. For this book, that number is now 125,000 persons from over 900 churches. As was the case then, the vast majority of these must remain unnamed because the contribution was an anonymous, though very personal sharing of their thoughts through a series of questions they chose to answer. This makes it difficult to speak in any possessive way about the discoveries in this book. As I keep saying, it is not so much what I have discovered, but what we have discovered together. Sadly, churches have systematically ignored these voices for far too long.

However in the midst of a multitude too great to number, a few names are important to mention. I want to thank Susan Niemi of Huff Publishing Associates for ably shepherding this book to completion and Marti Naughton for the terrific design.

It is always important to have the support of critical thinkers who will read early versions of a manuscript, make invaluable suggestions, and then take their place squarely in your corner. These precious folks include James Pence, Rev. Rebecca McClain, Keli Rugenstein, Jim Hanna, Jim Fenimore, Barry Frey, Susan Czolgosz, and Nancy Devor. I am especially grateful for Jim Pence who has worked tirelessly to carry the work of organizational intelligence into the succession planning in his own creative way.

The members of the Northeast Collaborative of Samaritan Counseling Centers, individually and as a group, are invaluable to me both as friends and colleagues. I am strengthened as I bring them to mind.

A special thanks goes to Robyn Strain who managed the source discovery for this book and made available the database for this analysis.

By taking the helm at Holy Cow! Consulting, Emily Swanson has not only contributed to my health, but also allowed me to "go below deck" and write this book. The fact that she is my daughter makes this a double blessing.

My wife, Shawn, continues to support my purposes in the world in ways that keep me grounded and mostly sane. Though now retired from health care management, her commitment to evidence-based approaches to make the treatment of adults and children as effective and painless as possible is inspiring. Her philosophy of supporting health rather than simply treating illness motivates me to carry those ideals over into organizations.

When I think that all these gifts are expressions of the pure grace of God, I run out of words.

J. Russell Crabtree
July 4, 2015

Contents

Foreword

I first heard the term "paradigm shift" in 1981 at a national conference for college English professors at the University of Michigan. On that occasion, we humanists were introduced to Thomas Kuhn's *The Structure of Scientific Revolutions* (1962) and the Kuhn Cycle, a way of looking at scientific progress.

> Kuhn challenged the world's current conception of science, which was that it was a steady progression of the accumulation of new ideas. In a brilliant series of reviews of past major scientific advances, Kuhn showed this viewpoint was wrong. Science advanced the most by occasional revolutionary explosions of thought so large they must be called new paradigms. From Kuhn's work came the popular use of terms like "paradigm," "paradigm shift," and "paradigm change."[1]

The theme of the conference was "Literacy in the Eighties," and the organizers were introducing us to the concept of *writing across the curriculum* as a paradigm shift in the teaching of college composition—the idea that writing could and should be taught throughout the curriculum by professors in all disciplines. Writing is a tool for learning, they argued, and students will learn to write more effectively and creatively if they practice writing beyond what they can possibly do in an English class. For years thereafter, the Michigan conference was cited as influential in the way the teaching of writing was revolutionized in colleges and universities. For the rest of my career in higher education, I hearkened back

---

1 http://www.thwink.org/sustain/glossary/KuhnCycle.htm

to the Michigan conference as a turning point in my understanding of literacy and of paradigm shifts.

Four years later, I attended a conference at the University of South Carolina based on the release of an October 1984 report from the National Institute of Education titled "Involvement in Learning: Realizing the Potential of American Higher Education." The seven authors of the report were all recognized as great leaders, and their work grabbed attention in the popular press as well as educational journals. Their focus on achieving excellence in student learning outcomes was hailed at the time as a paradigm shift in the philosophy of higher education:

> Much is known about the conditions under which student learning and growth can be maximized and about the methods and benchmarks by which these changes can be measured, even though the extent to which any one student benefits from these conditions depends on many immeasurable factors. But our colleges, community colleges, and universities rarely seek and apply this knowledge in shaping their educational policies and practices. We contend that the quality of undergraduate education could be significantly improved if America's colleges and universities would apply existing knowledge about three critical conditions of excellence: (1) student involvement, (2) high expectations, and (3) assessment and feedback.[2]

I still have a copy of this report on my bookshelf because I find that the three "critical conditions of excellence" apply in many of life's circumstances and in all kinds of organizations, including churches! The paradigmatic contexts of this report may seem surprising in retrospect. Was it really news to educators that students are more engaged in learning when they are involved, have high expectations, and receive timely feedback? It may not have been news, but it certainly initiated a radical shift in thinking about teaching and learning. Many of my academic colleagues scorned the view that student learning outcomes were all that important, especially since (as they argued) students don't always know what they don't know much less what they do know. "How will outcomes

---

2 http://www.jstor.org/stable/3446902?seq=1#page_scan_tab_contents

be measured?" they asked. "And to what end?" Revolutionary changes often generate fierce opposition.

I regret that the assessment movement in education deteriorated into the "no child left untested" approach in colleges and schools, but I embrace the notion that human beings crave involvement in shaping their futures, that we respond to high expectations, and we appreciate honest feedback that helps us improve. The 1980s produced a spate of reform reports that forced us to look deeply into our assumptions, to explore cognitive, affective, and behavioral aspects of teaching and learning, and to be intentional about curricular and pedagogical change. I have forgotten a good deal about most of the conferences I attended between 1981 and 2006 during my tenure as a professor and dean, but I remember these two. And, it is the recollection of the influence of these paradigm shifts that occurred to me when I read *Transition Apparitions*.

Russ Crabtree and I first worked together on a strategic planning process with a congregation in Minnesota in 2010. As I became familiar with him and his work, I thought at the time (and still do) that he is a "paradigm shifter." As one of the early adopters of the practice of congregational assessment, Russ showed that how people *feel* about their church turns out to offer important insights into the vitality of the church. These insights, when examined analytically, yield helpful intelligence about the organization, which in turn provides guidance for discerning strategies, initiatives, and plans. I count the *Church Assessment Tool* (known by all users as the CAT) and the other instruments Russ created for Holy Cow! Consulting as his first paradigm shift.

How many times I served on church councils and wondered how people would *react* to our decisions! How few times I thought about discovering what people were thinking and feeling in advance of making those decisions. We operated under the old assumption that we were elected to leadership because people trusted us to decide on their behalf, and our task was to communicate our decisions effectively to "bring them along." I think about generations of pastoral call committees who completed congregational profiles based on impressions, anecdotes, and hearsay. And I wonder how many pastors could have benefited from the kind of organizational intelligence collected by the CAT as they were discerning whether to leave their current positions or accept offered ones.

Just as the assessment movement in education brought fundamental change to teaching and learning, the assessment tools from Holy Cow! Consulting have created new ways of understanding church cultures and describing the sources of vitality and/or confusion. They have encouraged new ways of thinking that have triggered the kind of "revolutionary explosion of knowledge" about churches that Thomas Kuhn refers to as paradigm shifts in science. After five years of working with these assessment tools, I am more convinced than ever that the pathway to increased congregational vitality begins with the collection of organizational intelligence and with the enlightenment that comes from making public the thoughts and feelings of church members.

I count the second paradigm shift as represented by the publication of three Crabtree books that have revolutionized the way we think about planning in churches. In *The Elephant in the Boardroom: Speaking the Unspoken about Pastoral Transitions* (2004), Russ and coauthor Carolyn Weese reshaped the way congregations approach pastoral transitions. The inside flap of the hardcover edition accurately describes this book:

> Using assessment tools and quizzes, the book walks church leaders through the process of identifying their particular church's culture type and creating a succession plan that will meet their congregation's needs. Firmly rooted in biblical principles and the best management thinking, *The Elephant in the Boardroom* puts the focus on health, asset building, and resiliency. Its many illustrative examples from real-life situations and solid explanations offer elders, deacons, board members, and other lay leaders a how-to manual for planning, preparing, and executing a leadership transition.[3]

Since its publication in 2004, *The Elephant in the Boardroom* is often cited for its innovation and its utility as a tool for helping congregations design and implement successful pastoral transitions. *NeXt: Pastoral Succession That Works* (William Vanderbloomen and Warren Bird, 2014) and *Transitional Ministry Today: Successful Strategies for Churches and Pastors* (edited by Norman Bendroth, 2015), two recent notable contributions to the literature, make reference to the groundbreaking influence of *Elephant* in the area of pastoral transitions. Field manuals based on *Elephant* have had widespread use in congregations around

---

3 Weese, Carolyn and J. Russell Crabtree, *The Elephant in the Boardroom: Speaking the Unspoken about Pastoral Transitions* (Jossey-Bass, 2004).

the country, allowing Russ, Carolyn, and those of us who have been trained in evidence-based succession planning to apply the knowledge base from *Elephant* to specific congregational settings. Most of the succession planning work I have done begins when pastors and lay leaders read *Elephant* and become curious about an asset- and health-based approach to pastoral transitions.

In *The Fly in the Ointment: Why Denominations Aren't Helping Their Congregations and How They Can* (2008), Crabtree applies the tools of evidence-based planning to the work of regional associations. This book challenges conventional wisdom about the role of associations, such as dioceses, presbyteries, synods, and conferences, and offers a blueprint for transforming themselves and their denominations into vital and effective organizations. It is filled with examples from data collected in congregational assessments and illustrations of the many ways that "culture trumps strategy" often dooming congregational planning efforts to failure. The thesis of *Fly* is that transformational redevelopment of associations is central to congregational vitality.

Having worked in Lutheran, Episcopalian, Presbyterian, and United Church of Christ churches since 2007 in a variety of consultant roles, I am convinced that Russ's argument in *The Fly in the Ointment* deserves more attention and support than it has received. Regional associations everywhere seem to me to be struggling with questions of identity, purpose, and resources. People in the pews everywhere are functionally clueless about the mission and goals of their own regional associations. And my experience suggests that the good people, clergy and lay, who work in regional associations are looking for paradigm shifts to bring greater satisfaction, energy, and morale to their organizational lives. *The Fly in the Ointment* will challenge them, and their assumptions about their real work, in the same ways that *The Elephant in the Boardroom* helped pastors and churches "speak the unspoken" about pastoral transitions. My belief is that shrinking financial resources will eventually drive regional associations to evidence-based assessment of their vitality and perhaps to the realization that regional partnerships between and among those associations from different denominations may generate new and creative thinking about their own transformations. "Transformation requires memory fused with a new context and a heart of discovery,"[4] Russ wrote in the preface to *Fly*. The paradigm shifter is, as usual, ahead of his time when it comes to regional associations.

---

4 Crabtree, J. Russell, *The Fly in the Ointment* (Church Publishing INC, 2008).

The third Crabtree book is *Owl Sight: Evidence-Based Discernment and the Promise of Organizational Intelligence for Ministry* (2012). In my endorsement for the book, I wrote: "For those of us who care about the future of faith-based organizations, *Owl Sight* is a lamp unto our feet." It has been that, and more. Feedback from my succession planning clients is that this book is a necessary complement to *The Elephant in the Board Room* with its greater focus on the concepts and uses of organizational intelligence (OI) and its going beyond the mechanics of assessment processes to delve into the "spiritual labor required in taking a deep look in the mirror."[5] These clients tell me that they read *Owl Sight* and the *Vital Signs* report from their CAT surveys in tandem for real-time insight into their church culture, as well as practical support for understanding their information. My dog-eared copy always accompanies me on the road for on-site meetings with succession planning teams.

The revolutionary leap forward initiated in *Elephant* finds refinement in *Owl Sight*. Years of data from hundreds of churches provide the context for helpful generalizations about church cultures and patterns of evidence with predictive value for planning. From *Owl Sight*:

> We can now gain a clear understanding of the quality of member experiences in our churches and the critical factors for improving them. . . . For that incredible creature that is the namesake of this book, owl sight is not an optional ability that makes life interesting; it is his key to survival. Without it, he is destined to the scraps of food left by others on the forest floor. For the effective church leader in the information age, organizational intelligence is not optional either. It offers the capacity to see more clearly into the hearts of people to lead them to love and serve God at a time when other powers have far less noble purposes in mind.[6]

---

5 Crabtree, J. Russell, *Owl Sight, Evidence-Based Discernment and the Promise of Organizational Intelligence for Ministry* (Magi Press, 2012), 49.
6 Ibid., 206-07.

Both in content and style, *Owl Sight* resonates with clergy and lay leaders who want to see more clearly into their own hearts and to discern the vocation of their congregation based on evidence collected from the very people whose efforts and energy will heed that calling. Working from the specific to the general, Crabtree endows the concepts of OI with vivid illustrations gleaned from the experiences of thousands of participants in CAT assessments. I cannot imagine someone reading this book and NOT understanding the importance of paying attention to the quality of the experience members of congregations are offered. Actually paying that attention, of course, is a separate matter. Those who choose to do so have their footsteps on the path lighted by this delightful lamp.

The third paradigm shift is *Transition Apparitions*, in some ways a re-imagination of the vision of *Elephant* and in other ways a revolutionary adjustment to it—as in an "occasional revolutionary explosion of new knowledge." I know a bit of the story behind the story of *Apparitions*. Russ and I were talking about a 2012 article by Dan Hotchkiss, "Unconventional Wisdom: Whither Interim Ministry" posted on the Alban at Duke Divinity School website. Hotchkiss mentions how *Elephant* changed our thinking about pastoral transitions, especially in the use of interim ministers:

> Doubts about the interim idea have not gone away. Carolyn Weese and Russell Crabtree, in *The Elephant in the Boardroom* (Jossey-Bass 2004), complain that the "prevailing stream of thinking about leadership transitions tends to be illness-based. A pastoral transition is treated like a terminal diagnosis" (p. 19). Ouch!
>
> A morbid emphasis on "wounds and weaknesses," say Weese and Crabtree, forces congregations into a supine, patientlike dependence on the expertise of denominational officials and interim ministers. Instead, Weese and Crabtree recommend that governing boards take a more active role and engage in advance succession planning modeled on corporate practices. Especially in larger congregations, the promise of a swift and seamless leadership transition has considerable appeal.
>
> In congregations as in corporations, transition planning is much easier to advocate than to carry out successfully. The

governing boards of some large, conspicuous congregations have put transition plans in place only to find that, when the time comes, their chosen leader lacks the broad support needed for successful ministry.

Whatever the merits of their particular suggestions, Weese and Crabtree call needed critical attention to some aspects of Alban's early work on transitions. Some interim ministers do rely rather heavily on the Kübler-Ross grief model—which is a bit dramatic in most situations. The most effective interims, I find, balance openness to grief feelings with an appreciative approach to congregational strengths, and bring a broad and flexible portfolio of skills and concepts to the work.

. . . I still believe in interim ministry, though after forty years, I agree with Norman Bendroth that it's overdue for some rethinking. What is best for pastoral-sized congregations differs from what works in larger ones. Weese and Crabtree's criticism of the "illness-based" approach has merit—though the fact that I prefer to see myself as healthy doesn't mean I am.[7]

Intrigued by the proposition that interim ministry is "overdue for some rethinking," Russ began poking around in the Holy Cow! Consulting database and then turned (as he always does) to careful, systematic analysis of the data. He began rethinking his own thinking about pastoral transitions and came away absolutely convinced, as he said to me, "we need a new model." So he designed it.

One way of looking at *Transition Apparitions* is by studying its genealogy. The integration of biblical principles and management thinking for pastoral transitions in *Elephant* begat the vision of transformational associations focused on developing healthy, vital congregations in *Fly,* which begat the promise of organizational intelligence for enhancing the quality of ministry in *Owl Sight,* which begat the creation of an uncertainty-agency approach that focuses on the four essential elements of congregational sustainability: mission, stewardship, giftedness, and empowerment. The DNA of this genealogy is organizational intelligence. Its head is evidence-based discernment. Its heart is leading people to love and serve God.

---

7   http://danhotchkiss.com/whither-interim-ministry/

I write this as a "foreword" to this important work, but it is "afterward" that I find to be most important in dealing with the body of Russ Crabtree's work. I have often heard him say that in the church "we over teach and under train." That's another way of saying we often end up with words and concepts with no idea how or clear intention to do things differently. It's always what we do afterward that counts. In the conclusion to *Apparitions* he offers nine specific implications of the new model that require thought and action. The ball is in our court. In his onsite work with congregations, I have watched him create competence and confidence that they can implement the plans he has helped them develop, afterward. In his transition out of the leadership of Holy Cow! Consulting, he provided the framework for ongoing growth and development of congregational assessment, afterward. The only way we know if the paradigm has shifted is if we know what to do, afterward.

James L. Pence, PhD
President, Walkalong Consulting

Introduction

The transition from one leader to the next is an important season in any organization's life. Over the last forty years, a wide variety of approaches and nomenclature has been developed to address pastoral transitions in faith communities ranging from vacancy consultants, vacancy supply pastors, interim pastors, intentional interim pastors, transition teams, and succession planning.

Far and away, the predominant model for managing pastoral transition has been the utilization of an interim pastor (rector, minister, priest, depending upon the denomination). It has been generally assumed in any pastoral transition that an interim pastor would be called or appointed who would serve during the one-to two-year period required to call the next pastor. Alban consultant Dan Hotchkiss articulates this approach in his article "Whither Interim Ministry?"

We filled the great majority of full-time ministry positions with full-time, full-year interims, some of whom had special training and certificates. We saw the change of clergy leadership as a critical moment in a congregation's life, an opportunity to rethink everything: program, leadership, strategy, and purpose. It is also an emotional transition, similar to grief. A well-trained interim minister, engaged for a year or more, provides the support and counsel congregations need in order to move through it successfully. One of our strictest rules was that when the interim year (or two) was over, the minister had to leave. As for many other national and regional church bodies, for us interim ministry was an almost unquestioned good.[1]

One of the important contributions that the interim ministry movement has made to the church is an emphasis on the actual experience members were having in their congregations. Interim pastors started paying attention to what members were thinking and feeling during a pastoral transition. They found Elizabeth Kubler-Ross's stages of grief a helpful way of framing and attending to the needs of members based upon how they were feeling. Implicit in much of the methodology of interim ministry is the simple affirmation that experience matters.

A focus on the experience of church membership represented a significant change. Previously, church leaders tended to value loyalty, duty, and ecclesiastical connections, all summed up in an annual report featuring "count data," that is, what could be externally counted: people, dollars, and facilities. Interim ministry was reflecting a shift that focused on relationships and experiences with a much more conversational approach to ministry concerned with realities better spoken than counted: thoughts and feelings.

About the same time, this shifting emphasis on member experiences was reflected in the development of a number of assessment instruments that gave members an opportunity to communicate their thoughts and feelings to leaders in a more systematic way. Hartford Seminary developed a number of instruments under the heading of Congregational Assessment Inventories. Natural Church Development, TAGG (Toward a Greater Good), and Willow Creek

---

1 http://danhotchkiss.com/whither-interim-ministry/

have all developed assessment instruments. In addition there was a spate of denominational instruments. One of the earliest efforts was that of Dr. Grayson Tucker of Louisville Presbyterian Seminary in the late 70s resulting in what he named *A Church Planning Questionnaire.*

Surprisingly, the interim ministry movement never linked its focus on member experience with a comprehensive approach to *assess* member experience. This has left the movement vulnerable to a variety of uncertainties and even criticisms of its ministry, some justified, some not. It has also robbed it of the data that would allow interim pastors to customize their approach to different contexts. As a result, the movement has become somewhat ideological in its tone resulting in a one-size-fits-all methodology.

Instead of embracing assessment as an element consistent with its methodology, the interim movement has often joined forces with an establishment still committed to loyalty, duty, and position in resisting the collection of information on the kinds of experiences members were having during transitions. As a result, little research has been conducted on interim ministry. Hotchkiss makes note of this curiosity:

> Norman Bendroth, a network-certified professional interim, surveys the ferment and experiments afoot among members of the Interim Ministry Network. To date, Bendroth observes— and so far as I have been able to determine, he is right—no one has mounted a serious, objective study to evaluate whether interim ministry reduces conflict, improves ministerial selection, lengthens subsequent ministries, or improves congregational self-knowledge or effectiveness. Given the impact of the widespread use of interim ministry in a denominational system, this is an odd omission that some social scientist should remedy.[2]

A comprehensive evaluation would gauge the state of the church before and after a particular approach, as well as the longitudinal impact as measured by the state of the church and satisfaction of the next pastor after the first few years of service. Holy Cow! Consulting is not in possession of the data that would allow this kind of important analysis.

---

2 Ibid.

However, the organization does have an extensive data set consisting of responses from over 125,000 members in over 900 churches, many of whom were engaged in a pastoral transition, and some of whom utilized an interim pastor. This study is aimed at getting a glimpse into those churches and their experience with the interim pastors who served them.

In this study, three sets of data represented in Figure 1 were used. It is important to understand that this is not longitudinal data collected on individual congregations assessed at multiple points along the transition timeline. This is aggregate data collected from churches in these different contexts.

The first block of data consists of churches that were non-transitional. Because every church will eventually go through the next pastoral transition, these are referred to as "prior to transition." There are 662 churches in this portion of the database with about 82,000 respondents.

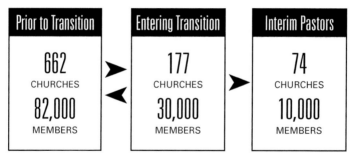

Prior to Transition	Entering Transition	Interim Pastors
662 CHURCHES	177 CHURCHES	74 CHURCHES
82,000 MEMBERS	30,000 MEMBERS	10,000 MEMBERS

FIGURE 1 Data Sources

The second block of data consists of churches "entering transition." These were churches that ran the transition module, which is typically run early in the process either before an interim pastor is in place or shortly after. This module consists of a set of questions designed to assess how members will respond to a pastoral transition. There are 177 churches in this portion of the database, with about 30,000 respondents.

The third block of data consists of churches with "interim pastors." These are churches that have had an interim pastor in place for at least six months or more. This is generally ten months to a year after the resignation of the former pastor, so the church is well into the pastoral transition at this point and is able to give informed answers to questions about the work of the interim pastor.

Following are several assumptions in this analysis that I believe are reasonable:

- There are many factors in the resignation of a pastor. Some retire. Some leave to take a larger responsibility. Others resign because of difficulties in the pastoral relationship of one kind or another. For churches "entering transition" their characteristics are both (a) the result of the pastor's resignation and (b) factors that may have caused the resignation. That is why the arrows in the diagram point both directions. It is impossible from the data to tell how much one is influencing the other.

- The aggregate data of churches "entering transition" provide a profile for a typical church that is valid. Clearly churches vary from one to another. Nonetheless, there are patterns that are valid for that population of churches.

- The standard practice for churches today is to utilize an interim pastor during a pastoral transition. There are exceptions, but they are statistically insignificant in the database. Therefore, we can establish patterns that can be generalized since most churches will move from "entering transition" to "interim pastor." Therefore, the arrow points in one direction. (This is another way of saying that self-selection errors are manageable.)

The results of this study are nothing short of astounding—thus the audacious title of the book. In articles that are now appearing and through conversations with several interim pastors, I am discovering a fresh openness to different ways of thinking about pastoral transitions. As with all of us, old thought patterns are hard to break.

The word *apparition* is used in reference to something that exists in perception only. Many of the key assumptions of the interim ministry enterprise remain in spite of the fact that much has changed on the religious scene. In contrast to thirty years ago, information is now accessible that previously was difficult or even impossible to collect.

Following are the apparitions that will be addressed in the chapters of this book:

APPARITION #1

Pastoral transitions traumatize congregations
much like the death of a spouse.

APPARITION #2

After the initial trauma of a pastoral
transition, churches gradually recover under
the ministry of an interim pastor.

APPARITION #3

Poor performance by interim pastors
is the primary reason churches have
difficult pastoral transitions.

APPARITION #4

Under the leadership of interim pastors, conflict
levels in congregations usually go down.

APPARITION #5

Congregations grow impatient during
pastoral transitions for no good reason.

APPARITION #6

Members explore other churches during
a pastoral transition because they have difficulty
dealing with their former pastor's resignation.

APPARITION #7

With the exception of the search
committee, members want to move to the
sidelines during a pastoral transition.

APPARITION #8

Churches with long-term pastors always
require long-term interim pastors.

APPARITION #9

The changes that an interim pastor
introduces during a pastoral transition help
a congregation become more flexible.

APPARITION #10

All churches deal with pastoral transitions
in basically the same way.

As you read on, you will see that all these are, in fact, false. Enjoy the surprising ride.

CHAPTER ONE

Pastors As Dead Spouses?

It is the theory that determines what is observed.

—ALBERT EINSTEIN

APPARITION #1

Pastoral transitions traumatize congregations
much like the death of a spouse.

On the face of it, it makes sense to frame the relationship of a pastor to the congregation as an analogy to marriage. Marriage is a relationship. Pastor and congregation are in a relationship. The marriage is protected by promises. The pastoral relationship is protected by promises. Husband and wife are called to love one another. Pastor and congregation are called to love one another. Husband and wife are called to bear fruit. Pastor and congregation are called to bear fruit.

It follows that the end of a pastoral relationship is like the death of a spouse. This model makes the dynamics of loss and grief the primary pathway for understanding what is happening in a pastoral transition. Once that step is taken an entire developmental structure emerges: the stages of grief. In his article "Whither Interim Ministry," Rev. Dan Hotchkiss notes a shift in interim ministry that occurred with the publication of Elisabeth Kubler-Ross's work.

> Transitional ministries were not new, of course. They had existed under many names, and other consultants like Lyle Schaller had encouraged churches to use interim ministers—but this was something different. Equipped with new ideas like the "stages of grief" made popular by Elisabeth Kübler-Ross, interims helped congregations talk about what they were experiencing. The emerging discipline of group dynamics helped interims to dignify the transition time as an occasion for important work, rather than a mere time of "vacancy" to be endured.[1]

Anecdotal conversations with interim pastors over the years confirm this basic pastoral orientation that extrapolates the individual experience of loss to that of a congregation. Some interim pastors have said that the primary goal of interim ministry is to help members learn how to grieve so that they can carry grief skills over into other areas of loss in their lives.

Once a grief-recovery model is adopted, there are a number of implications that rapidly follow:

- **Grief recovery doesn't happen quickly**. The rule of thumb is that a grieving person will need to walk through all the seasons of the year as a minimum in the healing process. Applied to congregations, this means that a church will need to have an interim pastor on board for *at least* a year.

- **The recovery period for grief lengthens depending upon the length of the marriage.** Applied to a congregation, pastoral transitions following long-term pastorates will require longer-term interim pastors.

- **Grief introduces an element of incapacitation to decision-making.** Just as individuals are counseled not to make large decisions in the first year after the death of a spouse, congregations may need to put major decisions on hold until a new pastor is on board.

---

1 http://danhotchkiss.com/whither-interim-ministry/

- **The services of an interim pastor are required to minister to the congregation during this period of loss.** Just as individuals cannot be their own "grief counselors," congregations cannot minister to their own feelings of loss.

- **If individuals do not appropriately tend to their grief, they will not be able to enter into another lasting relationship.** Congregations that do not address the grief of their loss will likely carry that into the next pastoral relationship where it will be unconsciously played out. This will result in an "unintentional interim."

The grief-recovery model has all the advantages of being practical, comprehensive, and intuitive. But does it really describe what happens in a church during a pastoral transition?

In fact, does it describe what really happens when a spouse dies? In a study by Boerner, Wortman, and Bonanno titled *Resilient or at Risk? A 4-Year Study of Older Adults Who Initially Showed High or Low Distress Following Conjugal Loss,* researchers followed the reactions of ninety-two men and women who lost spouses to death. See Figure 1.1.

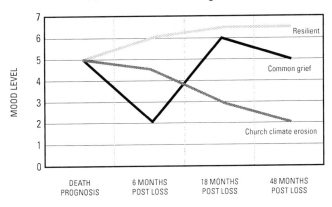

FIGURE 1.1 Patterns of Mood Change after Loss

Of those individuals, only 11% followed the "common grief" pattern with immediate shock, decreased mood that bottomed at six months, then returned to baseline at about eighteen months. However, the most common pattern was what the authors described as "resilient." Here is what they discovered.

A typical resilient wife who loses her husband will experience a depression of mood as she realizes he is dying (death prognosis). After his death her mood tends to recover. Over time, she will heal gradually and her spirits will lift. The researchers found this pattern 50% of the time.

If a pastoral transition is like other losses similar to a death, the expectation would be that the climate of the congregation exhibits a similar pattern: an erosion of morale at the announcement of a pastor's resignation compared to what it had been prior to the announcement. (In some cases, the erosion of morale will precede the resignation and be a precipitating factor. For our purposes, it really doesn't matter. A period of lower morale surrounds the resignation.) Subsequently we would expect to see a long period of gradual improvement. Is this what the research showed?

It isn't. What we observe in churches is a "climate-erosion" response. There is indeed a negative impact on vitality (mood) around the resignation announcement, but instead of gradual recovery over time, there is an accelerating erosion of vitality. The rest of this book explores the various dimensions of this pattern.

There are two key indicators of congregational vitality: satisfaction and energy. Satisfaction and energy are different but related factors.

For many people, the word *satisfied* has an unseemly quality to it because they associate it with self-satisfaction and it smacks of conceit. The word actually has its roots in the Latin *satisfacere,* which means "content" and *satis*, which means "enough."

In actual experience, for churches where members indicate a high level of satisfaction, the community usually reflects the Hebrew *shalom,* an expansive term that includes completeness, wholeness, health, peace, welfare, safety, soundness, tranquility, prosperity, perfectness, fullness, rest, harmony, and the absence of agitation or discord. Contrary to common belief, the research indicates that high satisfaction is never achieved by simply pandering to the self-interests of members. It is more accurately a *shalom* created by a number of components that combine to produce a sense of wholeness.[2]

2 Crabtree, J. Russell, *Owl Sight: Evidence-Based Discernment and the Promise of Organizational Intelligence for Ministry* (Magi Press, 2012).

The satisfaction level in a congregation was determined by asking members to respond to the statement: *On the whole, I am satisfied with how things are in our church.*

The responses of nearly 82,000 persons from about 662 churches prior to a pastoral transition, showed that 59% of respondents were clearly satisfied (strongly agreed or agreed), 34% were on the fence (tend to agree or tend to disagree), and 7% were clearly dissatisfied (strongly disagree or disagree). See Table 1.1.

Overall Satisfaction

	CHURCHES PRIOR TO TRANSITION	CHURCHES ENTERING TRANSITION
Clearly disagree	7%	9%
On the fence	34%	38%
Clearly agree	59%	53%

TABLE 1.1 Changes in Satisfaction Due to Transition

To determine the satisfaction level of churches entering a pastoral transition, the data was typically collected from churches approximately four months to six months after the resignation of the former pastor.

Note that the primary impact of entering a pastoral transition is not dissatisfaction but ambivalence. The satisfaction level drops about 6%, most of which shifts to on the fence. This makes sense. In a pastoral transition, some members are going to adopt a wait and see attitude. However, it is also important to observe that entering a pastoral transition does not have a substantial *negative* impact on how satisfied members feel compared to a typical church that is not facing a pastoral transition.

These and other data suggest a picture in stark contrast to what we would expect to see if a pastoral transition were analogous to a death. Rather than generating a significant level of pain or negativity, pastoral transitions tend to produce uncertainty.

Now we turn our attention to energy. In its Latin and Greek roots, the word *energy* does not have quite the material, physical connotation that energy has today, but is nuanced in the direction of work or force of engagement. This is how the word is understood in this context about congregational health and vitality. A high-energy church is one where members experience a compelling purpose or message combined with a high level of engagement, in contrast to a church where members are simply watching others or going through the motions of religious activity. Energy is distinct from satisfaction. You may have a car that evokes satisfaction (you love its shape, color, interior) . . . and is totally out of gas (energy). Sometimes folks are in a church that they sincerely love (they love the people, the liturgy, the history, the mission, and so forth), but they are out of energy. Conversely, people can be very energized about their engagement in a particular aspect of a church and yet quite dissatisfied with how things are being run overall. Satisfaction tends to be an operational quality. Energy tends to be more about purpose, meaning, and the capacity for action.[3]

The energy level in a congregation was determined by asking members to respond to the statement: *It seems to me that we are just going through the motions of church activity. There isn't much excitement about it among our members.* The question is negatively worded; agreement with the statement indicates lower levels of energy. The comparison between churches prior to transition and entering transition is found in Table 1.2. In contrast with satisfaction, the shift is more clearly negative for churches entering transition compared with churches prior to a transition. This makes sense if a congregation has the understanding that it is simply marking time until the next pastor can be recruited and settled.

Overall Energy (Just going through the motions)

	CHURCHES PRIOR TO TRANSITION	CHURCHES ENTERING TRANSITION
Clearly disagree	43%	40%
On the fence	43%	43%
Clearly agree	15%	17%

TABLE 1.2 Changes in Energy Due to Transition

---

3 Ibid.

Finally we turn our attention to an area where we would expect a pastoral transition to have the largest impact of all: worship. Members responded to the following statement: *The worship services at our church are exceptional in both quality and spiritual content.*

The comparative results for churches prior to a pastoral transition and churches entering a pastoral transition are found in Table 1.3.

Once again the shift is relatively small, and the change is not so much toward dissatisfaction with worship, but toward ambivalence.

Worship Satisfaction

	CHURCHES PRIOR TO TRANSITION	CHURCHES ENTERING TRANSITION
Clearly disagree	4%	5%
On the fence	33%	36%
Clearly agree	62%	59%

TABLE 1.3 Changes in Worship Satisfaction Due to Transition

These and other data suggest a picture in stark contrast to what we would expect to see if a pastoral transition were analogous to a death. Rather than generating a significant level of pain or negativity, pastoral transitions initially tend to produce ambivalence. As members reflect on their level of satisfaction, sense of energy and purpose, and worship, there is likely a part of them that feels excited for new possibilities and another part that feels anxious about what is going to happen next. The anxiety side of ambivalence can produce emotions that are similar to grief. Here the similarity ends. When someone loses a spouse that is loved, there is limited excitement for the new possibilities that now present themselves.

The ambivalence stage of a change process is an important precursor to attitude formation. As time goes on, folks on the fence will tend to fall one way or the other. If decisive action is taken build toward the opportunity side of the ambivalence, more positive attitudes will be formed. If not, organizational entropy is likely to erode the climate.

Alternatively the grief-recovery model would suggest that even small impacts should gradually lesson over time during a pastoral transition. Time is the great healer. In the next chapter, we will see if that happens.

APPARITION #1

Pastoral transitions traumatize congregations
much like the death of a spouse.

FINDING

Ghostbusted.

CHAPTER TWO

Getting Better All the Time?

The most challenging job of a leader
is intercepting entropy.—MAX DE PREE

APPARITION #2

After the initial trauma of a pastoral transition,
churches gradually recover under the ministry of an interim pastor.

As previously noted, churches experience relatively small changes in morale at the beginning of a pastoral transition, mostly in the form of an increased amount of ambivalence and "marking time." If action is not taken, ambivalence erodes into a more negative climate. In a grief-recovery model of pastoral transitions, the church should grow stronger with the passage of time much as an individual will recover after the death of a loved one as months pass. Is this what we see in our research?

**Instead of a recovery process, we are now seeing
the ambivalence-erosion pattern emerge.**

In the first chapter, two groups of churches were compared: a group of churches prior to a pastoral transition and a group of churches entering a pastoral transition (typically four to six months after the resignation of the former pastor). This chapter looks at the status of churches that have had an interim pastor in place for six months or more using the same aspects of church climate: satisfaction, energy, and worship.

After six months or more into the transition under the tenure of an interim pastor, there is a significant change in satisfaction. See Table 2.1. Not only has the number of members who are clearly satisfied declined significantly, and the number of persons on the fence increased significantly, but the number of persons who are clearly dissatisfied has increased above 10%, a threshold that usually indicates a significant level of polarization. This degree of polarization usually indicates a significant level of conflict, a topic that will be explored in a subsequent chapter.

Overall Satisfaction

	CHURCHES PRIOR TO TRANSITION	CHURCHES ENTERING TRANSITION	WITH INTERIM PASTOR SIX MONTHS OR MORE
Clearly disagree	7%	9%	11%
On the fence	34%	38%	44%
Clearly agree	59%	53%	45%

TABLE 2.1 Changes in Overall Satisfaction with an Interim Pastor at Six Months

Declines in satisfaction of this magnitude are important because they begin to put the church at a comparative disadvantage with other churches. Churches already have relatively low satisfaction scores compared with competing organizations like public libraries and yoga centers. Two-thirds of the churches in a community will have higher overall satisfaction scores than a typical church in transition with an interim pastor.

In a grief-recovery model, we might surmise a return of energy with the passage of time; a depressed mood is energy sapping. For a while, people just go through the motions of living, but then a sense of purpose returns. This is not observed with pastoral transitions.

In churches with interim pastors who have been in place for six months or more, rather than a recovery in the energy level of the church, there is further erosion. See Table 2.2. At this point one in five members clearly believes the church is simply going through the motions, a significant increase over churches prior to a transition. Nearly one-half the members are on the fence, and less than one-third disagree "that there is a lack of excitement in the church."

Overall Energy (Just going through the motions)

	CHURCHES PRIOR TO TRANSITION	CHURCHES ENTERING TRANSITION	WITH INTERIM PASTOR SIX MONTHS OR MORE
Clearly disagree	43%	40%	32%
On the fence	43%	43%	48%
Clearly agree	15%	17%	20%

TABLE 2.2 Changes in Energy with an Interim Pastor at Six Months

The typical church with an interim pastor and ten months into a pastoral transition (four months from the resignation of the former pastor plus six months into the tenure of an interim pastor) has a significantly lower level of energy than most churches in its surrounding community. Combined with the lower than average satisfaction noted earlier, the typical church with an interim pastor is slipping into lower levels of morale as time passes rather than "recovering."

How members feel about worship is one of the best predictors of satisfaction in a church. A decline in the member perceptions of worship generally signals a corresponding decline in morale. In the short term it is not surprising that worship scores should drop. In no other area of the church's life is the literal voice of the pastor so engraved into the neural pathways of the minds of members. Every worship service led by the voice of a different preacher is a reminder of that loss.

Again, one might imagine that with the passage of time, members would "recover" from that loss and begin to view worship more positively. Instead, we see a situation illustrated by the data in Table 2.3 on page 30.

Worship Satisfaction

	CHURCHES PRIOR TO TRANSITION	CHURCHES ENTERING TRANSITION	WITH INTERIM PASTOR SIX MONTHS OR MORE
Clearly disagree	4%	5%	5%
On the fence	33%	36%	40%
Clearly agree	62%	59%	55%

TABLE 2.3 Changes in Worship Satisfaction with an Interim Pastor at Six Months

Once again the decline is not represented in more folks feeling negative about worship. The entire shift is from the category "clearly agree" to "on the fence." As noted previously, this suggests that the primary issue for churches in a pastoral transition is not the recovery from grief, but dealing with ambivalence.

Figure 2.1 summarizes the trend in churches as they make their way through a pastoral transition. Changes in average scores are relatively small at the beginning, but the decline accelerates over time, especially in the areas of satisfaction and energy. Instead of a recovery process, we are now seeing the ambivalence-erosion pattern emerge that was described in Chapter 1.

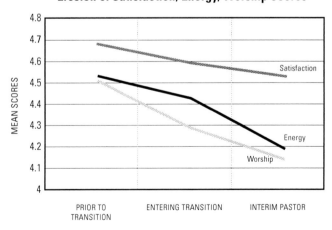

FIGURE 2.1 Trajectory of Satisfaction, Energy, and Worship during Transition

It is important to realize that the constellation of emotions associated with the anxiety side of ambivalence will be similar to those associated with grief. When a family taking a vacation by car is lost for any period of time and their physical well-being comes into question, members are going to go through denial (we're not lost), anger (that this is happening), guilt (we should have prepared better), and sadness (for the opportunities we are missing and the way we are treating each other).

The acceleration of losses within the tenure of a typical interim pastor raises a question that must be met head on: Is it the interim pastor's fault?

APPARITION #2

After the initial trauma of a pastoral transition, churches gradually recover under the ministry of an interim pastor.

FINDING

Ghostbusted.

CHAPTER THREE

Taking It on the Chin

There is nothing more deceptive than an obvious fact.

—Arthur Conan Doyle, The Boscombe Valley Mystery

APPARITION #3

Poor performance by interim pastors is the primary reason
churches have difficult pastoral transitions.

If key indicators begin dropping so dramatically for churches after the interim pastor arrives, it would seem a reasonable conclusion that the problem can be traced back to the interim pastor.

Let's be honest here. One of the coffee break conversations at pastoral conferences features a statement that sounds like this: "Many interim pastors are folks who were not able to make it as settled pastors. They don't have the skills or motivation to sustain a healthy congregation. I just hear too many stories of churches going downhill after the arrival of an interim pastor."

Sociologists who explore these kinds of questions point out the fallacy of confusing correlation with causation. Just because two things happen at about the same time doesn't mean that one is actually causing the other. The classic example is that of fires and fire engines. A person doing a study of house fires may regularly observe that every time there is a house fire there is a fire engine—and come to the conclusion that fire engines cause fires!

So let's address the question directly: Is the primary reason that vitality levels in congregations decline so sharply during a pastoral transition the performance of interim pastors?

This question will be explored by reviewing three areas of the interim pastor's work: communication, listening, and preaching to determine:

- How effective are interim pastors compared to non-transitional pastors?

- How important is the performance of interim pastors in these areas to the vitality of the church?

Interim pastors are as effective in the areas of communications and listening as non-transitional pastors, but somewhat less effective as preachers.

Leadership is a critical skill for effective pastors. Even if interim pastors are effective preachers, they also need to be effective at helping a church move forward in meaningful ways.

There are many dimensions to leadership, but one of the most critical during a pastoral transition is the ability to communicate effectively. Transparency gives members a feeling of control that is an essential antidote to anxiety.

Communication is about more than information. It needs to help keep members connected to one another during a time when folks tend to drift away. Members were asked to respond to the following statement: *Our pastor communicates with people in a way that keeps us informed and connected.*

Once again we can compare settled pastors, pastors of churches entering transition, and pastors of churches with interim pastors for six months or more. See Table 3.1. This data indicates that congregations actually score interim pastors about the same as the typical non-transitional pastor and significantly higher than the former pastors of churches entering a transition. It is possible that the members of churches entering a transition give lower marks to the communication of former pastors due to the inevitable suddenness of a resignation announcement. Members realize that their pastor has been in conversation with search committees from other churches, usually for some time, and has not let them know. Alternatively, lower performance in the area of communication could have been a factor in the pastor's resignation. Either way, leaders should expect that members will typically reflect on the communication performance of a former pastor less positively at the beginning of a pastoral transition.

Pastor Communicates Effectively

	CHURCHES PRIOR TO TRANSITION	CHURCHES ENTERING TRANSITION	WITH INTERIM PASTOR SIX MONTHS OR MORE
Clearly disagree	5%	11%	4%
On the fence	26%	33%	27%
Clearly agree	69%	56%	68%

TABLE 3.1 Changes in Pastor's Communication with an Interim Pastor at Six Months

Interim pastors as a group rate just as highly as non-transitional pastors in their communication. How important is this to satisfaction and conflict? Communication has a modest impact on overall satisfaction.

Listening skills and the ability to listen are important in any leadership position. Given the emotional elements of a pastoral transition, we might assume it is especially important for interim pastors.

Listening requires more than accurately determining the facts of a situation; it is also important to tune into feelings. To get at that skill, members were asked to respond to the following statement: *When conversing with a person, our pastor listens for feelings, as well as words, and treats feelings as important.*

The results are found in Table 3.2 on page 36. This appears to be an area where interim pastors shine. More folks are clearly positive regarding the listening skills of interim pastors compared with those of churches entering transition, but are also slightly more positive than non-transition pastors. An emphasis on pastoral skills, particularly listening skills, is not surprising, especially given the history of interim ministry. Anecdotal conversations with interim pastors confirm their pastoral orientation.

Pastor Listens for Feeling As Well As Facts

	CHURCHES PRIOR TO TRANSITION	CHURCHES ENTERING TRANSITION	WITH INTERIM PASTOR SIX MONTHS OR MORE
Clearly disagree	4%	9%	3%
On the fence	22%	29%	22%
Clearly agree	74%	62%	75%

TABLE 3.2 Changes in Pastor's Listening with an Interim Pastor at Six Months

Interim pastors tend to be much more fluent in the psycho-social aspects of pastoral transition than in transitional preaching or transitional leadership. Some indicate that the primary goal of interim ministry is to help members learn how to grieve so that they can carry grief skills over into other areas of loss in their lives. Rarely do we hear the opposite perspective, that pastoral transitions are times to teach members how to successfully navigate other transitions in their lives (which are legion).

How important is listening to satisfaction levels in a church? It has a smaller impact on overall satisfaction than communication.

Preaching is the other area of focus. In a typical church, most members generally feel positive about a pastor's preaching. The majority of members in almost all churches generally agree with the statement: *In preaching, our pastor engages people with a message that enriches their lives in the world.*

The question was constructed to clearly focus on the preaching of the pastor and his or her ability to engage people. If interim pastors are less capable than settled pastors, this is one of the first areas where we would expect to see a decline. Instead, we see a situation illustrated by the data in Table 3.3.

Preaching That Engages Members

	CHURCHES PRIOR TO TRANSITION	CHURCHES ENTERING TRANSITION	WITH INTERIM PASTOR SIX MONTHS OR MORE
Clearly disagree	4%	8%	5%
On the fence	22%	29%	27%
Clearly agree	74%	63%	69%

TABLE 3.3 Changes in Preaching with an Interim Pastor at Six Months

The significant dip for churches entering transition can reflect situations where pastors leave due to problems in the pastoral relationship, or it might reflect disappointment of members that the pastor is leaving them.

Overall, members rate the preaching of interim pastors at a lower level than non-transitional pastors. Interim pastor preaching scores are lower than 64% of pastors in non-transitional roles. This is not a huge difference, but it is enough that members will experience a change that will be disappointing to some.

Again, the shift in scores for interim pastors is not from feeling positive to feeling negative, but from feeling positive to on the fence. The percentage of folks who are clearly positive about the preaching drops 5% from non-transitional to interim pastors, but nearly all the shift is to the fence, that is, ambivalence.

How significant is the impact of preaching on vitality levels? In pastoral transitions, it has about the same impact as communication.

This suggests that interim pastor training might place more emphasis on effective transitional preaching.

We are now prepared to answer the question regarding the relative performance of interim pastors over the trajectory of a pastoral transition in these three areas: communication, listening, and preaching. See Figure 3.1.

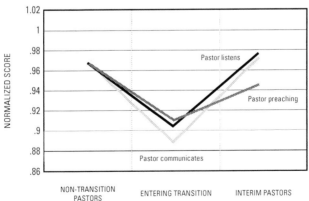

FIGURE 3.1 Perception of Pastor Skills at Various Stages of Transitions (normalized)

There is the familiar dip in the perception of former pastors as members entering a transition evaluate their pastors retrospectively, shortly after the pastor has left, then a more positive evaluation of interim pastor performance. Interim pastors are as effective in the area of communication and listening as non-transitional pastors, but somewhat less effective as preachers.

We are also prepared to answer the second question: How important are these skills in explaining the drop in satisfaction scores during a pastoral transition? Taken together, they explain about 25% of that decline. While substantial, it is clearly not the whole story.

While there are always individual exceptions, it appears that preaching, communication, or listening skills in interim pastors are important, but they cannot explain the *degree* of decline in morale that we see in the trajectory of churches going through a pastoral transition.

There is another possibility: neither lay leaders nor interim pastors have the necessary tools to effectively navigate a pastor transition. As explained later in this book, the problem may lie with the model used to train interim leaders.

Before leaving the topic of interim pastors, there is another question: What is the impact of interim pastors on conflict levels? That is the subject of the next chapter.

APPARITION #3

Poor performance by interim pastors is the primary reason churches have difficult pastoral transitions.

FINDING

Ghostbusted. Mostly.

CHAPTER FOUR

Fighting Words

Things may come to those who wait,
but only the things left by those who hustle.

—*ABRAHAM LINCOLN*

APPARITION #4

Under the leadership of interim pastors,
conflict levels in congregations usually go down.

hurch consultants have developed a fairly sophisticated approach to gauging church conflict. There are five levels ranging from level one where the conflict is seen as a problem to be solved to level five where it is intractable.[1] One of the tasks of a church in a pastoral transition is to deal with remedial issues, that is, to correct or address a problem carried over from the past. Conflict is one of these.

It is a cardinal rule that a conflicted church will need an interim pastor to assist in dealing with the conflict prior to the arrival of the next pastor. The assumption is that during the tenure of a skilled interim pastor, the level of conflict will be reduced. If that were true, then we would expect the level of

---

1 http://www.uucr.org/LEADERSHIP_FOLDER/LevelsOfConflict.htm

conflict in churches to go up shortly after the pastor's resignation to account for those churches where there were problems related to the pastoral relationship. Then we would expect conflict levels to begin to recede after the interim had been on board for a significant period of time. Is that what we actually observe?

In order to gauge the level of conflict, we asked members to respond to this statement: *There is a disturbing amount of conflict in our church.*

This question was constructed to focus on members' experience of conflict rather than on the conflict itself. All relationships have conflict that can be constructive and illuminating. It is when members begin to experience conflict as disturbing that it begins to have a negative impact.

Note also that the question is negatively worded, that is, it is desirable for folks to disagree rather than agree with it.

The data from the study is found in Table 4.1 In a typical, non-transition church, about 11% of respondents clearly agree that they are disturbed by the amount of conflict, with just over one-third on the fence and about one-half clearly disagreeing. In the group of churches entering a pastoral transition there is a slight increase in the number of persons who are clearly disturbed, but also the familiar pattern of folks moving to the fence.

Disturbing Level of Conflict

	CHURCHES PRIOR TO TRANSITION	CHURCHES ENTERING TRANSITION	WITH INTERIM PASTOR SIX MONTHS OR MORE
Clearly disagree	52%	46%	34%
On the fence	37%	40%	46%
Clearly agree	11%	13%	20%

TABLE 4.1 Changes in Perceived Level of Conflict with an Interim Pastor at Six Months

This indicates that *most* churches entering a pastoral transition do not have major conflict issues that trigger a resignation. In addition it suggests that most pastors are "sticking it out," even in situations where there is significant conflict. This may be due to a number of factors including (a) a lack of opportunities, (b) difficulty in dealing with the sale of pastors' homes, and (c) spousal and other family commitments to a particular region. The lack of mobility of pastors may perpetuate situations where a poor fit between clergy and congregation generates low levels of vitality.

In the typical church, members are more disturbed by the level of conflict after ten months than they were when they entered the transition.

What seems equally clear is that congregations entering a pastoral transition give the former pastor significantly lower scores on peaching, communication, and listening. This could indicate poor fit or the need for pastoral coaching/continuing education rather than resignation.

At six months or more into the transition under the tenure of an interim pastor, there is a significant increase in the level of "disturbance." Notice the very large shifts at both ends. There has been a 75% increase in the number of persons who clearly agree that they are disturbed by the level of conflict, and a 33% decrease in the number of persons who disagree with that statement. This suggests that after six months of service provided by an interim pastor, the average church is dealing with a significant level of conflict that is much higher than churches with a non-transitional pastor and also higher than a church freshly entering a pastoral transition.

It is important to remember that these scores are aggregated data. Undoubtedly there will be situations where some conflict levels have been reduced during the tenure of an interim pastor and some situations where conflict levels have become significantly worse. Overall, the trend is clear. In the typical church, members are more disturbed by the level of conflict after ten months (six months or more with an interim pastor) than they were when they entered the transition.

What is actually happening here? There are several possible explanations. See Figure 4.1 on page 42.

First, it is possible churches that choose to have interims are less satisfied and more conflicted to start with. However, this suggests that churches have a choice. With the exception of very large churches with a retiring pastor engaged in a succession-planning model, most mid-sized and smaller congregations will call an interim pastor as a matter of course if they have the financial resources to do so. They are usually not presented with options by their middle judicatory.

Also, the data from 177 churches entering transition showed that their satisfaction and conflict levels were only modestly different from those of churches that were not in a pastoral transition.

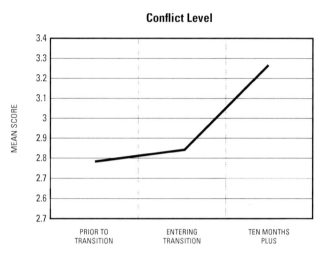

FIGURE 4.1 Perception of Disturbing Conflict at Various Stages of Transition

Second, it is possible that interim pastors are perceived as not performing well by members, which generates conflict. However, there is little correlation between member perceptions of an interim pastor and levels of conflict. The research indicates that only about 10% of a church's increase in conflict levels can be explained by the performance of the interim pastor.

Third, it is possible that interim pastors are initiating changes during a transition (such as increasing missional flexibility) that are painful in the short term but necessary for the long-term health of the church. Again, if this were the case we would expect to see interim pastors becoming the lightning rod for member dissatisfaction with decreased performance scores. But the data shows that interim pastors perform as well as other pastors with the exception of somewhat lower scores in the area of preaching. And a subsequent chapter will show that interim pastors are not particularly effective at increasing the flexibility of congregations.

Finally, it is possible that the pastoral transition model itself generates dissatisfaction and conflict regardless of the interim pastor. This leads to a broader conversation about conflict.

The subject of church conflict is too complex to engage in any detail beyond a few generalizations.

First, while there are a number of factors, the major sources of conflict are few. In a 2004 study of the causes of conflict published by *Christianity Today*, Carl Dudley, Theresa Zingery, and David Breeden found that control issues, vision/direction, and leadership changes were the top three.[2] See Figure 4.2.

Sources of Conflict

Control issues	85%
Vision/direction	64%
Leadership changes	43%
Pastor's style	39%
Financial	33%
Theological/doctrine	23%
Cultural/social differences	22%
Other	16%

Christianity Today survey, 2004

FIGURE 4.2 Sources of Conflict

Second, control issues tend to arise in response to the higher levels of anxiety that develop as one side of ambivalence. As examined in subsequent chapters, control is not simply the power to force a decision in a particular direction but giving members the feeling that they can have a positive effect through transparency, predictability, and influence. This is referred to as *agency*.

Third, vision and direction issues tend to arise in pastoral transitions, particularly in a model where a transition is understood as "a critical moment in a congregation's life, an opportunity to rethink everything: program, leadership, strategy, and purpose."[3] No other type of organization (library, hospital, coffee shop, mental health agency) undergoes such a sweeping reconsideration and potential discounting of its own history and learning than churches using this approach. By ignoring a congregation's organizational learning and subsuming

---

2 [2]http://faithcommunitiestoday.org/sites/all/themes/factzen4/files/InsightsIntoCongregationalConflict.pdf
3 http://danhotchkiss.com/whither-interim-ministry/

its identity under that of the former pastor, the degree of uncertainty is further exacerbated.

Finally, the *Christianity Today* article confirms the discovery from our own research: leadership changes themselves are sources of conflict.

Is this increased level of conflict due to anything specific, or is it simply a manifestation of generalized anxiety in the system? That question is addressed in the next chapter.

APPARITION #4

Under the leadership of interim pastors,
conflict levels in congregations usually go down.

FINDING

Ghostbusted.

CHAPTER FIVE

Just Because I'm a Hypochondric . . .

The first responsibility of a leader is to define reality.
The last is to say thank you.
In between, the leader is a servant.

—MAX DE PREE

APPARITION #5

Congregations grow impatient during pastoral transitions for no good reason.

. . . doesn't mean that I'm not sick. It is well-known that congregations grow impatient during pastoral transitions. Just as there are urban legends surrounding the capabilities of interim pastors, there are also conference coffee break conversations about congregations that go something like this: "How many times I have seen a congregation all in an uproar because the search process is taking too long! More often than not, it is the same congregation that needs to take a year or two to work through their issues or the next pastor is simply going to be an 'unintentional interim.'"

One gets the impression from such remarks that congregations are simply reacting to an irrational, generalized anxiety with no basis in fact. Is that actually the case?

Leaders seldom ask members what they intend to do during a pastoral transition, so they have no reliable information that will help them predict what will happen in the future. For example, if a significant number of persons indicate that they are going to explore other churches during a pastoral transition that could be a cause for concern.

The research actually did just that by asking members to respond to the statement: *During the pastoral transition, I am thinking about exploring other churches.*

A summary of the responses is found in Table 5.1. Notice that about three-fourths of respondents clearly disagree. Nevertheless, about 13% of respondents generally agree with the statement (tend to agree, agree, strongly agree). In other words, leaders *do* have something to be concerned about during a pastoral transition.

Thinking about Exploring Other Churches

	CHURCHES PRIOR TO TRANSITION
Strongly disagree	50%
Disagree	26%
Tend to disagree	12%
Tend to agree	7%
Agree	3%
Strongly agree	3%

TABLE 5.1 Member Intentions during the Transition, Exploring Other Churches

In general, worship attendance in mainline denominational churches is declining. See Figure 5.1. In our database, that decline in non-transitional churches is about 1% per year. During the period when a church enters a pastoral transition, that rate of loss accelerates slightly to about 4% per year. By the time the church has had an interim pastor on board for six months or more, the rate of loss increases to 12% per year. This means that on average churches in transition are losing worship attendance at a rate twelve times that of non-transitional churches.

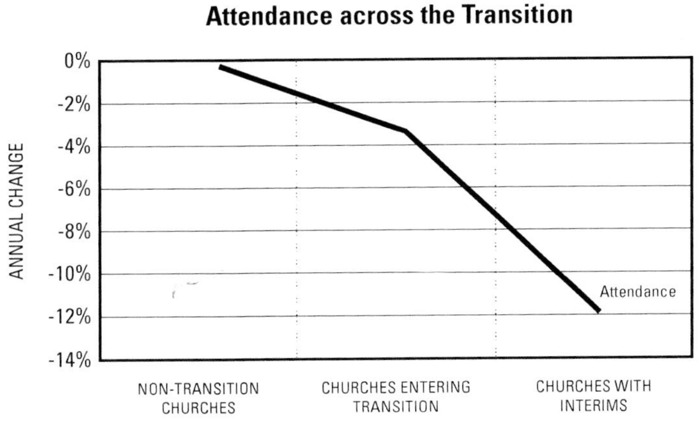

Attendance across the Transition

FIGURE 5.1 Changes in Worship Attendance

In a church with two hundred persons in worship, that represents a loss of twenty-four persons during a twelve-month interim and forty-eight persons during a twenty-four-month interim. This is enough to be visually noticeable to many members. In addition, some members will find it painful when they have personal relationships with the folks who drop out. For those members who are attuned to these losses in attendance the church will be clearly weaker; for those who are not attuned to the losses perceptions regarding the strength of the church will be different.

Worship attendance isn't the only concern. By the time a church has had an interim pastor for six months or more, the typical church is reporting a net drop in revenue of 7% per year. This is occurring at precisely the time when a church needs additional revenue to (a) fund a search process, (b) cover the costs of moving a pastor, (c) get the salary package of the pastor up-to-date, and (d) demonstrate to candidates that a church is on solid financial footing.

Taken together, the drop in attendance and revenue becomes a source of concern to some members as the pastoral transition stretches out weeks, months, and sometimes years. While some members may be able to exercise a degree of faith to leave the results to God, the stewardship concerns of others cannot be dismissed as irrational.

In fact, it appears that this polarization of views regarding the state and trajectory of the church is largely what is fueling the increasing levels of conflict as time goes on. These areas of polarization were discovered in the responses to several questions.

The first question is aimed at getting a sense of whether members perceive the church is stronger or weaker during the interim period. Members responded to the question: *When you think about the overall strength of the church now compared to the strength of the church just prior to the resignation announcement of your previous pastor would you say the church is (a) much weaker, (b) weaker, (c) about the same, (d) stronger, or (e) much stronger?*

About 35% of respondents in a typical church indicated that the church was clearly stronger (stronger or much stronger); 37% indicated the strength of the church was about the same; and 28% indicated the church was clearly weaker (weaker or much weaker). See Table 5.2. Certainly members have different perceptions of what is happening in a church being served by an interim pastor. However the fact that one in three members sees the church as stronger while one in four members sees the church as weaker indicates a degree of polarization that in and of itself can fuel conflict.

Is the Church Stronger or Weaker?

	CHURCHES DURING TRANSITION
Much weaker	6%
Weaker	22%
About the same	37%
Stronger	24%
Much stronger	11%

TABLE 5.2 Change in Church Strength Since Resignation

By examining how members felt about the pace of the transition, additional insight was gained. Members were asked to comment on the statement: *I am comfortable with the pace of our transition process including our search for a new pastor.*

This question correlates strongly with the perceptions of a weaker or stronger church. Just over one-half of respondents (51%) clearly agree that they are comfortable while 12% clearly disagree, and the balance is on the fence (37%).

In general, when more than 10% of the congregation is on the negative side of a system-wide question, it becomes a potential source of conflict.

Another potential factor in the perception of a weaker or stronger church is the degree to which members feel the church is adjusting to the loss of the previous pastor. Members were asked to respond to this statement: *At this point, I believe that the congregation has adjusted well to the loss of the former pastor.*

The question also correlates very strongly with the perception of a stronger or weaker church. Of the respondents, 56% clearly agree that the congregation has adjusted well while 7% clearly disagree, and the balance is on the fence (37%).

The pace of the transition and adjustment to the loss of the pastor tends to run in opposite directions from one another. Allowing time for people to adjust to loss slows down the pace. Quickening the pace runs the risk of bringing on a new pastor before members have had an opportunity to deal with their feelings of loss. The tension between maintaining an appropriate pace and giving members time to deal with loss is another source of conflict. Roughly twice as many members are uncomfortable with the pace of the transition as are those uncomfortable with the loss of the previous pastor.

Churches tend to be resilient communities that can endure a great deal of externally imposed short-term stress. Natural disasters such as storms and floods, accidental fires, and community crises tend to be shared experiences that provide opportunities for members to unify in common cause.

Surprisingly, over one-half of the increase in the conflict levels in churches in transition can be attributed factors within the transition process itself.

Churches do less well with internal stresses, especially when members have differing perceptions of what is actually happening. On some issues, difficulties can emerge when a relatively small, but committed, minority have perceptions that differ from those of the majority. With questions that are system-wide in their perspective, the impact ratchets upward when 10% of the congregation is on the opposite side from the majority. We call it the polarization threshold.

For each of the three questions in Table 5.3 (on page 50), percentages are listed of churches that are (a) above the 10% polarization threshold and (b) above the 20% polarization threshold.

Levels of Polarization on Key Questions

	PERCENT OF CHURCHES WITH 10% MINORITY OR MORE	PERCENT OF CHURCHES WITH 20% MINORITY OR MORE
Ready to follow the lead of the next pastor	17%	0%
Church has adjusted well to the loss of former pastor	30%	1%
Church is stronger or weaker since former pastor resigned	62%	28%

TABLE 5.3 Number of Churches Polarized on Key Questions

About one in six churches is polarized at the 10% level around the question of whether the church is ready to follow the lead of the next pastor. Roughly one in three churches is polarized around the question of whether the church has adjusted to the loss of the former pastor.

By far, the highest levels of polarization are seen in response to the question of whether the church is stronger or weaker since the former pastor resigned. Sixty-two percent of the churches are polarized at the 10% level; twenty-eight percent of the churches are polarized at the 20% level.

Surprisingly, over one-half (52%) of the increase in the conflict levels can be attributed factors within the transition process itself. The three largest contributors are:

1. the degree of polarization around the question of whether the church is stronger or weaker since the resignation of the former pastor

2. the degree of polarization around the question of whether the church has adjusted well to the loss of the previous pastor

3. the degree of polarization around the question of whether the church is ready to follow the leadership of the next pastor

This point is illustrated by examining two churches with interim pastors represented in the two tables that follow (Tables 5.4 and 5.5).

Church A has relatively low levels of polarization on the three key factors as measured by the percentage of persons who clearly agree or clearly disagree with the statement (removing the on the fence scores). As a consequence, only

11% of members indicate they are clearly disturbed by the amount of conflict in congregation suggesting a low conflict level.

Church A: Conflict Level Low

Percent of members clearly disturbed by the level of conflict: 11%

STRENGTH OF CHURCH	ADJUSTED TO LOSS	READY TO FOLLOW
Clearly weaker 14%	Clearly disagree 0%	Clearly disagree 0%
Clearly stronger 47%	Clearly agree 77%	Clearly agree 77%

TABLE 5.4 Sample Church with Low Conflict Levels and Low Polarization

In contrast, Church B has much larger levels of polarization around the three factors, particularly the perception of whether the church is weaker or stronger since the resignation of the former pastor. As a result, 30% of members are clearly disturbed by the amount of conflict suggesting a high conflict level.

Church B: Conflict Level High

Percent of members clearly disturbed by the level of conflict: 30%

STRENGTH OF CHURCH	ADJUSTED TO LOSS	READY TO FOLLOW
Clearly weaker 35%	Clearly disagree 15%	Clearly disagree 5%
Clearly stronger 44%	Clearly agree 51%	Clearly agree 52%

TABLE 5.5 Sample Church with High Conflict Levels and High Polarization

It has been a long statistical journey through this chapter, but the central theme is clear. The *primary* reason that conflict levels rise in a church is not due to a lack of appreciation for the work of the interim pastor, nor from the irrational generalized anxiety within the system, but by different reactions of members to what is actually happening in the church.

This is a pivotal moment in the life of a congregation. The initial ambivalence has deteriorated into a significant level of uncertainty. A valuable model of interim ministry must have a clear and effective way of addressing this issue.

The next chapter turns our attention to the question: "Why do members explore other churches during a pastoral transition?"

APPARITION #5

Congregations grow impatient during transitions
for no good reason.

FINDING

Ghostbusted.

CHAPTER SIX

Dear John, Oh How I Hate to Write

People say I give them hell.
I don't give them hell.
I tell the truth and they think it's hell.

— *HARRY TRUMAN*

APPARITION #6

Members explore other churches during a pastoral transition because they have difficulty dealing with their former pastor's resignation.

As discussed in an earlier chapter, members indicate what they will do during a pastoral transition with a fair degree of accuracy. This is especially true in their indication that they will explore other churches.

On average, about 12% of respondents generally agree with the statement that they will explore other churches during the pastoral transition; over 75% clearly disagree. Again, this varies widely from one church to another. For example, in one church, 47% of respondents indicate they will not explore other churches while in a second church that number is 93%! The first church needs a transition strategy with a major retention component while the second church can turn its attention to other transition issues, like learning about growth strategies it wants its next pastor to lead.

What makes the difference between Church A and Church B? One possibility is that members of a church with a long-tenured beloved pastor may be so dismayed at the thought of the church without him or her that they can no longer attend the same church. If that were the case, then we would see a relationship between the inclination of members to explore other churches and positive regard for the former pastor. In other words, the more positive that members felt about the former pastor's ministry (preaching, for example), the more likely it would be that they would explore other churches.

But is this what the data reveals?

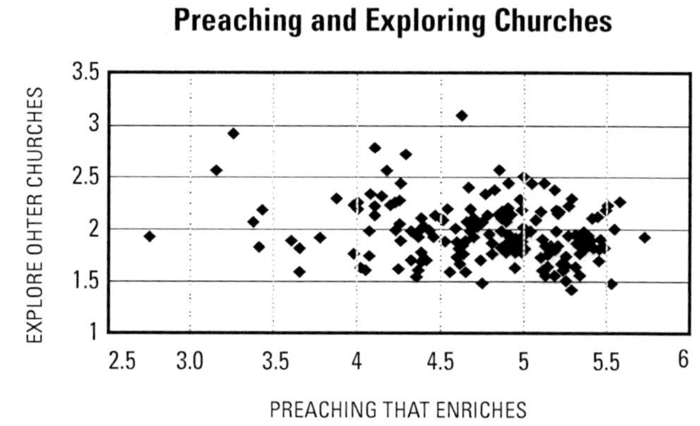

Preaching and Exploring Churches

FIGURE 6.1 Tendency to Explore Other Churches and Former Pastor's Preaching

Figure 6.1 plots the tendency of members to explore other churches in relationship to their evaluation of the preaching of the former pastor. If the graph looks random, that's because it is! There is virtually no relationship between those two factors. Respondents who are remembering a former pastor who was an outstanding preacher are no more likely to explore other churches than members remembering a mediocre preacher.

The reality is that there is very little relationship between how members feel about the former pastor's preaching, pastoral care, or leadership and their indication that they will explore other churches. Again, this challenges the assumption that member behavior in transitional churches is driven *primarily* by feelings of loss.

Let's examine some factors that have *virtually nothing* to do with why most people decide to explore other churches during a pastoral transition. Some of these are expected while others are quite surprising. For example, we might think that members who live further away would be more likely to explore a church closer to their home, but this is not the case. Apparently, members who are committed enough to drive past other churches, are also committed enough to see a pastoral transition through.

What is striking about these risk factors is that they are primarily focused on the atmosphere of the church.

Conversely, we might assume that members who have been in the church longer would be more committed to "stick it out." In fact, long-tenured members are no less likely to explore other churches than relative newcomers.

Since "participation breeds commitment," we might also believe that folks who are more involved beyond worship might be less likely to explore other churches. In fact, more involved folks are no more or less likely to explore other churches than those who only attend worship.

It is also surprising that the amount of giving to the church does not have some effect on the stability of attendance during a pastoral transition. This is the value of an evidence-based approach to pastoral transitions. It allows you to be surprised.

Other factors that appear to have little bearing on whether folks will explore other churches include (a) gender, (b) age, (c) ethnic background, (d) education, and (e) number of children in the household. One positive aspect of the insignificance of these factors is that they are very difficult to change. It is difficult, for example, to make someone younger or older as a retention strategy.

Next we can look at factors that are *somewhat predictive* of whether members are likely to explore other churches.

First, members who give higher priority to strengthening the way the church calls, develops, and supports leaders are also more likely to indicate they will explore other churches. One explanation is that these are folks who feel burned out, undeveloped, and underappreciated in their current faith community.

Members who give higher priority to reaching new members, especially families with children and youth, also are more likely to explore other churches. This could be because most mainline churches are struggling with this priority, and members may want to look for a faith community that is growing numerically.

Other factors that appear to have a *moderate impact* on whether folks will explore other churches include (a) wanting the church to give more attention to Christian education and formation, (b) being more concerned about the quality of relationships in the church, and (c) being more theologically conservative.

Leaders and members have control over *some* of these factors. While it may be difficult or undesirable to shift the theological perspective of the church, paying attention to relationships during a pastoral transition can pay significant benefits.

Members who indicate they will explore other churches are *significantly* more likely to also be less satisfied with the church overall and be concerned that members are simply going through the motions. The less vital the church, the more vulnerable it is to losing members during the pastoral transition.

Members who are more concerned with the quality of worship and think the church should be giving more attention to improving worship are also much more likely to explore other churches. Making sure the worship experience, including the preaching of the interim pastor, is as inspiring and engaging as possible is important to a retention strategy.

Exhibiting a disturbing level of conflict and a lack of willingness to resolve problems through mutual effort are surefire ways of losing members during a pastoral transition.

Finally, members who are less confident about the way decisions are being made, specifically the perception that leaders may not have genuine concern about how members are thinking, is also a significant factor in folks deciding to explore other churches.

What is striking about these risk factors is that they are primarily focused on the atmosphere of the church. The good news is that several are also largely within the control of the members. If members are leaving because they miss the previous pastor, there is little that can be done about that. And little can be done about members who are leaving because they live some distance from the church or have a higher level of education.

On the other hand, leaders and members *can* do something about the atmosphere in the church, the way leaders and members engage one another, the way they deal with conflict and disagreement, and the energy and purpose they bring into their faith community. Given these findings, an effective pastoral transition model needs to develop these as *protective* factors. By giving members a sense of control, leaders can better manage the church's vulnerabilities during a pastoral transition.

The next chapter looks at further evidence that members want to be meaningfully engaged during a transition.

APPARITION #6

Members explore other churches during
a pastoral transition because they have difficulty
dealing with their former pastor's resignation.

FINDING

Ghostbusted.

CHAPTER SEVEN

Put Me in Coach

The two enemies of human happiness
are pain and boredom.

—*ARTHUR SCHOPENHAUER*

APPARITION #7

With the exception of the search committee, members want
to move to the sidelines during a pastoral transition.

In most churches, members are assumed to play a relatively passive role during a pastoral transition. Depending upon the polity, the congregation may elect the search committee; other times it is appointed by the governing board. After the initial development of the search documents, all the action shifts to the search committee, which meets in closed, confidential sessions while members wait for the white smoke from the chimney, whatever form that takes.

There are sermons heralding the importance of waiting, of listening, of expectancy. With regard to the past, including the former pastor, members are counseled to grieve and let go. They may be discouraged from any significant decision-making until they are through their transition.

Ordained clergy go to seminary for years to study scripture, theology, and church history, and that is replicated at the congregational level through Bible studies and classes. Nothing like that usually happens with members or leaders during a search process. Interim pastors receive specialized training and even certification on managing pastoral transitions. None of this results in an equivalent, scaled down training for members, or even leaders for that matter, on how to serve effectively during a transition. Seldom are members given anything like, "Here are the three concrete steps we need every member to take to set the stage for our next pastor."

The typical transition process is built on assumptions that undermine a core theological concept: the priesthood of all believers. During ordinary time, members are told in a hundred different ways that they are the church, the body of Christ, the people of God, and that everyone is called to ministry. Suddenly, upon the departure of the pastor another, quite different, message is communicated: You are *not* the church. Your former pastor was the church. Now that he or she is gone, everything needs to be rethought. You thought the church was the people, who remain, who have developed capacities, and made commitments. That may all change depending upon the *style* of the next pastor. We need to wait for his or her arrival to know for sure.

Here we see one of the themes of this research: members need a sense of agency during a pastoral transition. Agency is defined as the capacity, condition, or state of acting or exerting power.

Is this theologically, psychologically, and spiritually sound? Is this what members want?

As churches entered a pastoral transition, members were asked to respond to the statement: *It could take a number of months to complete a pastoral transition. During that time I intend to be (a) much less involved, (b) less involved, (c) about the same, (d) more involved, (e) much more involved.*

Notice that this is the flip side of the question regarding exploration of other churches. Instead of looking at what could be framed as a *lack* of commitment to the congregation, it looks at the potential *increase* in commitment.

When the responses of almost 28,000 members were examined, here is what was discovered. See Table 7.1.

Anticipated Member Involvement

	CHURCHES PRIOR TO TRANSITION
Much less involved	1%
Less involved	3%
About the same	71%
More involved	20%
Much more involved	5%

TABLE 7.1 Member Intentions during the Transition: Involvement

Only 4% of the respondents indicate they will become less involved, roughly the same number who clearly agreed that they would explore other churches (6%). On the other hand 25% of respondents, one in four, indicate they would become more or much more involved.

What about helping with the pastoral transition itself? How willing are members to specifically engage with the work of helping the church navigate through this important time? Members were asked: *There are a number of additional responsibilities that may arise during the pastoral transition (for example, prayer, focus groups, committee work). Please indicate your level of availability to help with additional responsibilities as they arise: (a) much less available, (b) less available, (c) about the same, (d) more available, (e) much more available.*

This question gives us a window into the degree to which members see themselves as active participants or passive spectators of the transition process. When the responses were examined, this is what was discovered. See Table 7.2 on page 62.

Anticipated Member Availability

	CHURCHES PRIOR TO TRANSITION
Much less available	3%
Less available	7%
About the same	55%
More available	30%
Much more available	5%

TABLE 7.2 Member Availability for Transition Tasks

Of the members in a typical congregation, 35% see themselves as being more available or much more available to help with transition tasks. This is a stunning result! In a congregation with two hundred persons in worship, seventy of them want to help with the transition. Since search committees are typically no larger than five to ten persons, this means that over sixty persons want to make a contribution, but have no way to do so.

The underutilization of volunteers is a major problem among nonprofits in general. In a study cited in the *Stanford Social Innovation Review* it was found that "nonprofits rely heavily on volunteers, but most [leaders] do a poor job of managing them. As a result, more than one-third of those who volunteer one year do not donate their time the next year—at any nonprofit."[1]

Finally, we turn our attention to financial giving. Members of a church entering a pastoral transition responded to this statement: *There are a number of additional financial costs during a pastoral transition (for example, search costs, relocation costs, and so forth). Please indicate your anticipated level of giving during the transition.*

Responses are found in Table 7.3

---

1 http://www.ssireview.org/articles/entry/the_new_volunteer_workforce

Anticipated Member Giving

	CHURCHES PRIOR TO TRANSITION
Much lower giving	2%
Lower giving	2%
About the same	83%
Higher giving	13%
Much higher giving	0%

TABLE 7.3 Member Giving During the Transition

In the typical church, about 13% of members indicate they are willing to increase their giving *to support the pastoral transition* (not the general fund). However, this impulse is rarely tapped by a special appeal to help cover search and relocation costs. It is interesting to note that giving typically goes up as churches enter a pastoral transition, but then drops significantly during the tenure of an interim pastor.

By now you are probably noting a potential contradiction. Members are indicating they will become more involved, more available for transition tasks, and will give more money. But the behavior of a typical congregation six month later is such that there is lower attendance and reduced giving. What does this mean?

The data suggests that members enter into a pastoral transition with a level of ambivalence. There is a part of them that wants to become more engaged to help the church navigate through the transition process. There is another part of them that wants to wait to see what will happen . . . or even disengage.

This points to one of the themes of this research: members need a sense of *agency* during a pastoral transition.

Agency is defined as "the capacity, condition, or state of acting or exerting power." As will be discussed in a subsequent chapter, the major antidote to the negative impact of uncertainty in the church is the development of a sense of agency or power among the members. But what typically happens in a pastoral transition is that members are disempowered. This disempowerment is not intentional. It is a result of the failure to understand the need for member engagement that involves creating additional roles for members in tasks specific to the transition.

Nowhere does this need for engagement become more critical than in the church where a long-term pastor is retiring. We turn to that scenario next.

APPARITION #7

With the exception of the search committee, members want to move to the sidelines during a pastoral transition.

FINDING

Ghostbusted.

CHAPTER EIGHT

A Time for Every Purpose

Guests, like fish, begin to smell after three days.

—BENJAMIN FRANKLIN

APPARITION #8

Churches with long-term pastors always require
long-term interim pastors.

Whether you agree with it or not, Ben Franklin's proverb illustrates the complexity of relationships. You may not want to spend forever with some folks, even those you hold in great affection. In some churches served by long-term pastorates, members hold their beloved, seventy-year-old, thirty-year-tenured Pastor Smith in high esteem . . . but they are ready to move on to a different leader. All this is communicated in whispered tones with great anxiety about hurting Pastor Smith's feelings.

This runs counter to another maxim that is: churches with long-term pastors always require long-term, interim pastors.

How do we distinguish between a church that will have trouble letting go of a former pastor from one that is ready to move on? To get at this, members were asked to respond to this statement: *I am comfortable with the timing of a pastoral transition. I think it is time for a change.*

The question was intentionally blunt to surface any level of emotional discomfort with the transition. The responses of over 26,000 persons can be found in Table 8.1.

Comfort with Transition Timing

	CHURCHES PRIOR TO TRANSITION
Strongly disagree	8%
Disagree	10%
Tend to disagree	13%
Tend to agree	24%
Agree	26%
Strongly agree	19%

TABLE 8.1 Ready for a Change

About 17% are clearly uncomfortable, 45% are clearly comfortable, and about 37% are on the fence. This is a remarkable finding. It suggests that the portion of the congregation that finds a pastoral loss difficult to navigate emotionally may be smaller than we have thought.

Six months into the tenure of an interim pastor, often little progress has been made. When folks were asked if the church has adjusted well to the loss of the previous pastor, 56% clearly agree, 37% are on the fence, and 7% clearly disagree. The research shows that this has little impact upon the church *unless* the membership is polarizing around the question and becoming conflicted over their readiness to call a pastor.

In a typical church, a minority of folks is uncomfortable with the timing of a pastoral transition and will likely have significant emotional reactions. This appears to change slowly over time.

However the level of comfort with a transition varies greatly from one church to another. Consider Church A and Church B in Table 8.2.

I Am Comfortable with Pastoral Transition Timing

	OVERALL	CHURCH A UNCOMFORTABLE	CHURCH B COMFORTABLE
Clearly disagree	17%	64%	6%
On the fence	38%	27%	29%
Clearly agree	45%	9%	65%

TABLE 8.2 Ready for a Change

In Church A, nearly two-thirds of the members are clearly uncomfortable with the timing the pastoral transition. This church is going to require a substantial degree of support in dealing with their feelings of loss. It is likely that Church A will require the services of an intentional interim.

Church B is in an entirely different emotional position. Two-thirds of the members are comfortable with the timing; only 6% are uncomfortable.

As the data in the table indicates, we cannot make a blanket statement regarding feelings of loss that will apply to all churches in transition. In Church A we might anticipate that there is going to be a significant experience of loss that will need to be addressed in the transition. Speeding up the transition in this church will be disastrous. In Church B the situation is quite different. In this church, slowing down the pastoral transition will be extremely frustrating.

We might think that pastoral transitions in larger churches are more difficult. Surprisingly, there is virtually no correlation between church size and the level of comfort with a pastor's resignation. This suggests that the primary level of discomfort with a pastor's resignation is not the loss of a personal relationship, but the impact of the resignation upon the vitality of the congregation. It also suggests that a "grief model" of pastoral ministry may not be the best option for interim ministry in many cases. See Table 8.3 on page 68.

Comfortable with Pastoral Transition Timing by Size

	WORSHIP ATTENDANCE (UNDER 200)	WORSHIP ATTENDANCE (200 TO 999)	WORSHIP ATTENDANCE (1000+)
Clearly disagree	20%	16%	19%
On the fence	36%	38%	39%
Clearly agree	45%	46%	42%

TABLE 8.3 Ready for a Change

Whereas size of the church and (I suspect) pastoral tenure have little impact on the level of comfort that members have with a pastoral resignation, the vitality of the church has a significant impact. This confirms what was stated above. What members are most concerned about in a pastoral transition is not a loss of the personal relationship to the pastor, but the loss of vitality in the church. Table 8.4 shows the level of comfort with the pastoral transition for the fifteen churches with the highest satisfaction and the fifteen churches with the lowest satisfaction in the database. Clearly the churches with the highest level of satisfaction have the lowest level of comfort with the timing of a pastoral transition.

Comfortable with Pastoral Transition Timing by Satisfaction Level

	ALL CHURCHES	15 CHURCHES WITH HIGHEST SATISFACTION	15 CHURCHES WITH LOWEST SATISFACTION
Clearly disagree	17%	31%	14%
On the fence	38%	43%	28%
Clearly agree	43%	26%	58%

TABLE 8.4 Ready for a Change

This suggests that an interim pastor philosophy built around conserving and expanding the vitality of the church is a better approach than one that helps a congregation deal with loss.

We are now back where we began. The question of whether a long-term interim pastor is needed in a church does not follow a formula but is dependent upon a number of contextual factors. Two of the most important factors are (a) the congregation's comfort with the timing of the pastoral transition and (b) the level of vitality in the congregation at the time of the transition.

The next chapter we will look at one of the critical components of vitality in any church: flexibility.

APPARITION #8

Churches with long-term pastors always require long-term interim pastors.

FINDING

Ghostbusted.

CHAPTER 9

Times They Aren't a Changin'

The secret of change
is to focus all of your energy,
not on fighting the old,
but upon building the new.

—SOCRATES

APPARITION #9

The changes that an interim pastor introduces during a pastoral transition help a congregation become more flexible.

One of the purposes of "an experienced intentional interim [is to] assess church health issues and help introduce and manage change in preparation for the new pastor."[1] Anecdotally, interim pastors speak about making small changes in worship on a regular basis that represent a departure from the practices of the former pastor. The hope is that these changes, small or large, will reduce in any rigidity that might make it difficult for a new pastor to give expression to his

---

1 http://www.convergemidamerica.org/blog/2014/03/8-reasons-call-interim-pastor

or her own particular style of ministry. By increasing the adaptability of the congregation, the risk of the next pastor becoming an "unintentional interim" is reduced by creating more distance in both time and experiences from the former pastor. It also opens the congregation to consider fresh approaches to ministry that might be more effective.

The research supports the fact that missional flexibility is critical to the vitality of a church. Missional flexibility is the ability of a congregation to make the changes necessary to achieve its vision in a particular context without needing to invest large amounts of energy managing internal conflict. Increasing the missional flexibility of a congregation is often an important transition task.

Is that what actually happens? Following are the responses of members to three questions that I believe are important measures of flexibility.

Members were asked to respond to the statement: *Our members welcome changes in worship.*

The question was constructed to provide a measure, not on the amount of change introduced into worship, but the attitude of members toward changes. If leaders are placed in a situation where they are regularly introducing changes into the worship life of a congregation that is unhappy with change, it will likely become a source of conflict. Remember mission flexibility has not been achieved as long as change is generating significant conflict. Table 9.1 shows what was discovered.

Welcome Changes in Worship

	CHURCHES PRIOR TO TRANSITION	CHURCHES ENTERING TRANSITION	WITH INTERIM PASTOR SIX MONTHS OR MORE
Clearly disagree	14%	16%	22%
On the fence	61%	62%	59%
Clearly agree	25%	22%	19%

TABLE 9.1 Welcome Changes in Worship

Notice that there is a small change in member responses from churches prior to transition and churches entering transition. The mean score on this question has dropped 3.5% between those two phases. However, ten months into the transition (six or more months after the interim arrives), the mean has dropped almost three times that amount: 10%.

**While increasing the self-awareness of a congregation
is a helpful step toward change,
it is insufficient by itself to create change.**

One way to interpret these scores is that the congregation is becoming more self-aware as it encounters the changes introduced by the interim pastor. As members become aware of their own discomfort, they realize that they may not be as open to changes in worship as they thought they were.

What about how much change is actually taking place in worship? Members were asked to respond to this statement: *We are willing to adapt our worship to the needs and circumstances of the people we want to reach in our local community.*

This question is also focused on changes in worship, but it is constructed to gauge the actual amount of change that is made in order to reach members of the community. Whereas as the question above was focused on the underlying attitude toward change, this question measures the amount of change introduced for a particular purpose.

The responses in Table 9.2 show the same general pattern: member perception changes little between the stages "prior to transition" and "entering transition." A more substantial decrease occurs six months into the service of an interim pastor. Again, this may be best explained as a growth in the self-awareness of the congregation.

Willing to Adapt Worship to Reach Community

	CHURCHES PRIOR TO TRANSITION	CHURCHES ENTERING TRANSITION	WITH INTERIM PASTOR SIX MONTHS OR MORE
Clearly disagree	8%	8%	11%
On the fence	49%	51%	56%
Clearly agree	43%	41%	33%

TABLE 9.2 Willing to Adapt Worship

Notice that more members clearly agree that the church makes changes to reach new people in the community (33%) than clearly agree that members welcome changes in worship (19%) in Table 9.1.

To get a read on how much change is introduced to meet the internal needs of members, members were asked to respond to this statement: *Our church changes its program from time to time to meet the changing needs of its members.*

The responses of members across the pastoral transition are found in Table 9.3. Notice that this question has the highest level of agreement and the lowest level of disagreement of any of the other three questions. This suggests that the typical congregation is more focused on making changes to meet the needs of members than on people it wants to reach in the community.

Changes Programs for Members

	CHURCHES PRIOR TO TRANSITION	CHURCHES ENTERING TRANSITION	WITH INTERIM PASTOR SIX MONTHS OR MORE
Clearly disagree	5%	6%	7%
On the fence	46%	49%	53%
Clearly agree	49%	46%	40%

TABLE 9.3 Changes Program for Members

In addition, the decline in the average score on this question across the pastoral transition is the lowest of all three questions. It would appear that members are learning that they are more likely to change to meet the internal needs of members than to reach out to those in their community.

The data from all three questions give a similar picture. Member perceptions of a congregation's flexibility do not increase under the ministry of an interim pastor. They decrease significantly. It is not likely that the interim pastor is training members to become less adaptable. One explanation is that members are discovering themselves to be less flexible than they believed. This increase in self-awareness is likely the result of their reactions to changes introduced by the interim pastor or by the simple fact that the interim pastor is a different person.

While increasing the self-awareness of a congregation is a helpful step toward change, it is insufficient by itself to create change. Change also requires clarity regarding desired goals, understanding why change is necessary to accomplish those goals, a commitment to changing behavior in concrete ways, and a willingness to use self-awareness as a way of forgiving oneself rather than a way of excusing oneself in moments of regression.

Question: How many Presbyterians does it take to change a light bulb?

Response: Who said anything about change?

The fact that members (of whatever denomination) can chuckle knowingly at that joke does not mean that they are prepared to make the necessary changes that make for missional flexibility. The changes that interim pastors make during their tenure are potentially a step in the right direction, but they must be combined with a more intentional change management approach at the member level than is currently happening.

APPARITION #9

The changes that an interim pastor
introduces during a pastoral transition
help a congregation become more flexible.

FINDING

Ghostbusted.

CHAPTER TEN

Jumping to Contusions

One of the most sincere forms of respect
is actually listening to what another has to say.

—*BRYANT H. MCGILL*

APPARITION #10

All churches deal with pastoral transitions in basically the same way.

Feedback loop: the element in a process that adjusts its operation according to differences between the actual and the desired outcome.

Everyone who cares about the mission of Christ's church wants the same thing from a pastoral transition—the calling of a pastor who is a good fit for who the church is and where it wants to go, stepping into a situation where the stage has been set for his or her success, and beginning ministry on a positive trajectory. That is the desired outcome.

The problem with most of the current approaches to pastoral transitions is that they have no feedback loop, that is, a mechanism that provides information that helps leaders make necessary adjustments to customize an approach to a particular situation. It is a bit like having a furnace in a home without a thermostat. The furnace runs at the same rate all the time putting out the same amount of heat. On some days the house will be much too hot. On other days it will be much too cold. On a few days when the temperature outside is within a very narrow range, the house will be perfect.

Without a good feedback loop, it is impossible to get an accurate picture of what is really going on in a congregation. This opens the door to a one-size-fits-all approach based on assumptions that may or may not be true. These assumptions often have painful ramifications upon the congregation, a "jumping to contusions." One of the findings that has jumped out in this study is the amount of variability there is from one church to another. For example, take this statement: *In the future, I believe the church should continue in the same overall direction that it has taken in the recent past.*

Table 10.1 shows the responses of members from two churches, Church A and Church B.

Church Needs to Continue in the Same Direction

	OVERALL	CHURCH A CHANGE COURSE	CHURCH B STAY THE COURSE
Clearly disagree	12%	49%	1%
On the fence	50%	38%	27%
Clearly agree	38%	12%	72%

TABLE 10.1 Changing Future Direction

The members of Church A clearly want to change course; roughly one-half of the members clearly disagree that the church should continue in the same direction.

The members of Church B clearly want to keep moving in the same direction that the church has taken in the recent past. Almost three-fourths of the members clearly agree with this statement.

A transition plan for Church A will be significantly different from Church B. The transition issues that need to be addressed for Church A include:

- Rethinking the church's mission, vision, and core values.

- Taking steps to explore the degree to which the church may be exhibiting a "slingshot" over-reaction that will create problems in the future.

- Examining potential system issues that are generating problems that need to be addressed.

- Providing interim leadership that can facilitate a process of this scope and stay long enough to see it through.

Issues that need to be addressed for Church B include:

- Taking steps to explore the degree to which the direction of the church may be linked to the former pastor and not owned by the congregation.

- Identifying any unique qualities of the congregation that might require training for the next pastor to function effectively.

- Clarifying the ways in which the next pastor will simply maintain what is currently in place and where the congregation would be open to leadership in new directions.

- Providing short-term interim leadership that can facilitate these tasks without "rethinking everything."

A similar exploration is required regarding the expectations of the next pastor. To get at this question, members were *not* asked what they wanted in the next pastor (which ends up sounding a lot like Jesus), but asked to respond to this statement: *I believe the next pastor we call should have approximately the same skills and responsibilities as our current pastor (for example, balance between preaching, administration, pastoral care, and leadership).*

Again, we will look at two churches that we will refer to as Church A and Church B. See Table 10.2.

Next Pastor Should Have the Same Skills

	OVERALL	CHURCH A SAME SKILLS	CHURCH B DIFFERENT SKILLS
Clearly disagree	14%	3%	50%
On the fence	38%	20%	36%
Clearly agree	49%	77%	14%

TABLE 10.2 Expectations for the Next Pastor

Each of these churches has different risks and opportunities related to attachment, idealization, reaction, and reinvention that will need to be reflected in the pastor profile developed by the search committee. There also may be issues related to pastoral expectations that need to be addressed in the transitions.

We have already seen how the members of a typical church want to be available to help with the transition process both with their time and their giving. This also varies widely from one church to another. Look at the data in Table 10.3 from two churches, Church A and Church B, and their availability to help with transition tasks.

Available to Help with Transition Tasks

	OVERALL	CHURCH A HIGH AVAILABILTY	CHURCH B LOW AVAILABILTY
Much less available	3%	0.0%	19.2%
Less available	7%	4.7%	19.2%
About the same	56%	44.2%	28.8%
More available	30%	44.2%	28.8%
Much more available	5%	7.0%	3.8%

TABLE 10.3 Two Churches and Availability Profiles

In Church A roughly one-half of the members are going to be more available to help with the transition with only 5% indicating less availability. In a church with two hundred persons in worship, the leadership needs to create one hundred meaningful roles to support the transition.

In Church B about a one-third will be more available, but more than one-third will be less available. This church will need to be careful with any new initiatives during the transition period. Again, each church needs a transition strategy tailored to its particular context.

There are roughly twenty different parameters that need to be considered in developing a transition plan, pastor profile, and start-up plan that is tailored to a particular church. However, it all hinges on having that thermostat that measures the atmosphere within the room.

APPARITION #10

All churches deal with pastoral transitions
in basically the same way.

FINDING

Ghostbusted.

CHAPTER ELEVEN

A New Model

I've missed more than 9,000 shots in my career.
I've lost almost 300 games. 26 times, I've been
trusted to take the game winning shot and missed.
I've failed over and over and over again in my life.
And that is why I succeed.

—*MICHAEL JORDAN*

B ased on the research that was presented in previous chapters, following is a summary of the trajectory of a typical church going through a pastoral transition.

The pastor announces his or her resignation, usually six to eight weeks before leaving either to serve another church or to retire. In a very small number of cases, a retiring pastor announces a year before leaving and the church enters a succession planning process. However, this is still relatively rare and happens more in larger churches.

Three to four months after a pastor announces his or her resignation, little changes in the climate of a typical church. There is no large increase in dissatisfaction though there is a level of ambivalence as a few folks move from being "clearly satisfied" to "on the fence." There is a small, but significant decrease in the energy level of the church with more people feeling that the church is simply marking time. With regard to conflict, the number of folks feeling disturbed remains about the same, though again, a few folks move to the fence.

About one-third of members indicate they are willing to be more available to help with transition tasks. A small, but significant group of people, about 15%, indicate they are willing to give more money to support the transition.

Most churches do not capitalize upon these opportunities. About 6% of members begin exploring other churches. Attendance drops slightly. Giving goes up slightly.

Emotionally, roughly one-half of the congregation is now comfortable with the pastor's resignation. A small but significant minority of about 17% is clearly uncomfortable.

Satisfaction with worship does not change appreciably though a few more people indicate they are now "on the fence," which is a theme for this early period of pastoral transitions.

Most churches going through a pastoral transition and can afford it will call an interim pastor. When looking at the church ten to twelve months after the former pastor's resignation announcement, things have changed significantly. Ambivalence has now eroded the climate and generated a level of uncertainty about what is happening in the church.

In a typical church, dissatisfaction levels have increased about 50% by this point, which is above the threshold where polarization becomes an issue. The energy level has dropped precipitously with twice as many people indicating the church is now simply "going through the motions."

Fissures begin to appear in how members perceive the state of the church during the transition. Roughly one-half of the members believe the church is doing as well as it was prior to the resignation announcement of the former pastor. Just over one-half of the membership feels the church is ready to follow a new leader, but the rest clearly disagree or are on the fence. Roughly the same situation exists regarding the adjustment of the congregation to the loss of the previous pastor with just over one-half clearly agreeing and the rest disagreeing or on the fence. About one-third of the members believe the church is stronger. Just over a one-quarter of members believe the church is weaker.

Those who believe the church is weaker are factually correct in this sense. Attendance is dropping at a rate of 12% per year. Giving is dropping at a rate exceeding 5% per year. This is happening at the very time when additional revenue will be needed to support the search and relocation process.

Differences in perspective on what is happening during the transition begin to increase conflict levels. Prior to the transition, about 11% of members were disturbed by the level of conflict. Now it is twice that.

The interim pastor is functioning just as well as any other pastor in listening and communicating, though he or she is probably not as gifted at preaching. As conflict levels go up, the interim pastor begins to communicate more but with little result. Communication about the process does not appear to be the primary issue.

The interim pastor is a new face with a new voice and style. He or she may intentionally (and courageously) try to introduce changes as a way of increasing the flexibility of the congregation in preparation for the next pastor. There is generally enough pushback for members to realize that they are not as open to change as they thought they were, but not enough to understand or commit to adaptive change.

On nearly every issue, more people are moving to the fence, and people on the fence are falling to the negative side of things. Members are increasingly uncertain about the state of the church and how they feel about it.

There are several different kinds of uncertainty that affect churches.

FIGURE 11.1 Types of Uncertainty for Churches in Transition

First, there is what is known as *state uncertainty*. State uncertainty is the inability of members to answer the question "What?" What kinds of experiences are our members having in our church? What are their perspectives on issues within the church? What are their aspirations for the church's future? State uncertainty arises because it is impossible in a church with more than about thirty-five persons in worship to understand what members are thinking by simply using an informal network of relational communication. For example, the research shows that it is virtually impossible for individual leaders to accurately estimate how members are experiencing the church at any given moment (see *Owl Sight*, pages 1–4).

Second, there is *effect uncertainty*. Effect uncertainty is the inability of members to understand the causes of certain events, to be able to answer the question "Why?" Why did the pastor resign? Was something wrong? Or when there are failures in a series of pastoral relationships, members may be thinking: Why does this keep happening to us? Why is the search process taking so long? Why are other churches growing but we aren't? Why are people leaving? Why is giving down?

Third, there is *result uncertainty*. Result uncertainty is the inability of members to predict the consequences of specific actions, to answer the question "What if?" What if we have a long-term interim pastor? Will that help us be ready to follow the next pastor's lead or will we lose momentum? What if we call a younger pastor? Will that help us attract younger members? Or will it dissatisfy older members? What if we call a pastor fresh out of seminary? Will he or she have more energy and fresh ideas? Or will inexperience create too many problems?

During a protracted pastoral transition, state, effect, and result uncertainties tend to increase. State uncertainty (what?) increases because members do not know what other members are experiencing in dealing with the changes that are taking place. Also, some members, leaders, for example, have access to information that others do not have creating a disparity in perspective between those who "know what is going on" and those who do not.

Effect uncertainty (why?) also increases over time. This is partly due to a confidential search process where search committee members cannot share why the candidates they are interviewing are not a good fit or why the process is taking so long when a candidate changed his or her mind and reversed a decision at the last minute leaving the committee to start over again. In larger churches, personnel committees cannot disclose why staff members have been asked to leave as part of the transition to the next pastor. Members may not understand why an associate pastor cannot be considered for the senior pastor position. In addition, they may not understand why attendance or giving is dropping. Is a drop in attendance due to the fact that members are exploring other churches during a pastoral transition or is it simply due to the season of the year, bad weather, or a general trend that is nationwide?

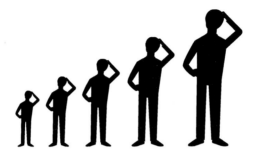

FIGURE 11.2 Uncertainty Grows Over Time in a Pastoral Transition

Finally, result uncertainty (what if?) also increases over time. As members become more uncertain (and often conflicted) about the state of the church, and as they also become more uncertain about why things are happening, they also lose confidence in their ability to predict what will happen next. In some cases they will regress to approaches that worked in the past but may not in the future. There is often a division between folks who want to conserve the past and others who want to try new things, but neither group can be totally certain that what they are proposing will be effective.

We know some things about the impact of uncertainty on an organization. In organizations where people do not have good alternatives, uncertainty tends to *increase* loyalty. Think of a community where the professional football team is rumored to be leaving. Members band together and rally to keep the team because there generally no other options for that particular professional sport in their community.

However, in organizations where members have multiple options, uncertainty tends to *reduce* organizational loyalty. Think of a department store where the opening time keeps changing. Shoppers are going to start going to the store down the block where they can count on a consistent schedule.

Unfortunately for churches, members have many options for church involvement, most of them with a settled pastor and a consistent leadership team. A decline in denominational loyalty has opened up even more options for members rattled by the uncertainty in their church during a pastoral transition.

The data suggests that a two-year interim will see a 24% decline in worship attendance. This means that in a worship space that was previously at capacity, one in every four pews will now be empty.

In addition, there are psychological effects caused by uncertainty. As with loyalty, these effects vary depending upon the situation and person.

For many persons, uncertainty creates a significant level of stress. Emotions that accompany uncertainty include anxiety, fear, worry, and sadness, some of the same emotions exhibited by people grieving a loss. However, not everyone has this reaction to uncertainty.

In a significant study by Bar-Anan, Wilson, & Gilbert it was found that for people having positive feelings about an experience, uncertainty tended to make the experience even more positive. For people having negative feelings about an experience, uncertainty tended to make the experience even more negative.[1]

Think of a movie that you are really enjoying, but at the end of the movie, things are left up in the air. The uncertainty at the ending makes the movie even more pleasurable for you. You hope there is a sequel. Now, think of a friend watching the movie with you who feels the movie is boring. The uncertainty at the end of the movie will make her like the movie even less.

Now think of members in a church. As they say, you can't please everyone. Some people will feel more positive about a church experience, some will feel more negative. The growing uncertainty in a church during a pastoral transition will tend to intensify positive and negative feelings. The result will be increasing levels of polarization and conflict.

This means that the key is to reduce uncertainty as much as possible for those who are experiencing it more negatively while maintaining enough openness in the process so that those who are feeling positively about a journey of discovery don't have all the "magic" sucked out of it.

One of the ways to help members of an organization deal with uncertainty is by increasing their sense of *agency*. In the broadest sense, agency is usually described as exercising influence or power in order to reach certain goals. When we speak about control, a governing board or individual in authority comes to mind. When we speak about agency, we are referring to something distinct.

---

1 *http://www.optimalfunctioning.com/psychology/feeling-uncertainty-intensifies-affective-reactions.html*

Agency is more than governance. There are basically three elements to agency: transparency, predictability, and influence.

Transparency is access to information that describes the entire system or an important subgroup of the system. Having a clear understanding of the perspectives, experiences, and aspirations of members as a whole is a critical element of transparency. Such information not only reduces state uncertainty (the what), it can also disclose patterns that reduce effect uncertainty (the why), as well as result uncertainty (the what if). This not only reduces uncertainty, it offers an element of agency to the typical member who feels that a few solitary, but influential voices may hijack the process.

Predictability is confidence that a particular course of action will have a desired result. When members feel that they can formulate goals in a plan that they can actually accomplish, and that those accomplishments are positive for the church, their level of uncertainty goes down. This has the additional benefit of engaging members in collective action that enhances cohesion and reduces polarization.

FIGURE 11.3 Taming Uncertainty: Transparency, Predictability, Influence

Influence is the capacity to have an effect. In general, most members do not want to serve in a governance role with all the attendant responsibilities. Most do not want to serve on a search committee either. However, many members want to play a role in supporting a pastoral transition—over one-third of the members in the average church. Engaging as many persons as possible in a variety of meaningful roles helps them deal with uncertainty.

Transparency, predictability, and influence have the benefit of reducing uncertainty. In addition they provide opportunities for members to have positive experiences. As already noted, uncertainty makes positive experiences even more positive. We don't want to try to eliminate all uncertainty, even if we could.

Taken together, these elements provide a framework for shaping a pastoral transition using an uncertainty-agency model, which is quite different from a grief-recovery model. Here are some aspects of a pastoral transition that emerge from this alternative model:

- Provide opportunities for as many "leaders" as possible to participate in guiding the transition process. These would not only include the governance board, but also staff members, other boards (trustees, deacons), committee members/ministry teams, association leaders, lay ministers, past leaders, search committee, and so forth. This not only increases influence, it encourages teamwork and reduces polarization.

- Collect organizational intelligence that gives insight into the entire congregation as well as significant subgroups such as governing boards and church staff. This enhances transparency with all its attending benefits.

- Formulate a vision for the transition. This provides a positive collaborative experience for the entire leadership body and emphasizes influence. Leaders often experience a mysterious coherence in this process, an experience that makes the positive experience even more positive.

- Facilitate a team identification of strengths within the church that leaders want to sustain across the transition. This focus reduces uncertainty and enhances corporate self-esteem.

- Assist the leadership team in developing concrete goals for the congregation in the areas of transition, search, and start-up that involve as many persons in the congregation as possible. This not only emphasizes the influence of members it also strengthens the predictability of setting goals and then achieving them.

- For congregations with low levels of missional flexibility, develop congregation-wide training on adaptive change that is linked to concrete participatory behaviors.

- Manage as much of the grief recovery process as possible by mobilizing resources extant in the congregation. This could include healing ministries, Stephen's ministers, lay ministries, calling teams, prayer teams, and so forth. This strengthens influence in a congregation through the power of a lay ministry affirmed in most Christian theologies.

The research suggests and our experience confirms that an uncertainty-agency model much more accurately reflects what happens in congregations during a pastoral transition. In addition, the model has practical implications that lead directly to concrete steps that sustain morale and reduce conflict.

Conclusion

"An organization has not really changed
until it does 90% of the right things
without even thinking about it."

—RUSS CRABTREE

In June 1948, the Bell Aircraft Company announced that test pilot Chuck Yeager had broken the sound barrier for the first time in the X-1A rocket plane. Yeager had actually accomplished this feat on October 14, 1947, but it had been kept secret until the following year.

Previous to that historic event, many aviators believed that a man was not meant to fly faster than the speed of sound, theorizing that transonic drag rise would tear any aircraft apart. Ironically, newspapers were debating the issue after it had already been accomplished, but not yet announced. It is humorous to imagine Chuck Yeager reading the newspaper to discover that what he had done was impossible!

I am frequently engaged by practitioners in conversations and debates about whether this different approach to pastoral transitions can succeed. Actually, an uncertainty-agency model has already been developed and implemented in about thirty churches or middle judicatories by Carolyn Weese, Russ Crabtree, and Jim Pence. While there is still much to be learned, the success rate of these transitions has been impressive as measured by short-term successes and participant satisfaction. We have seen no "unintentional interims" even in churches with long-term pastorates that did not utilize the services of an interim pastor. Other practitioners report similar improvements in pastoral transition success rates. A book detailing the nuts and bolts of evidence-based succession processes is due for publication in January 2016.

The implications of this model are significant.

- First, we need to significantly retool our current approach to interim pastor training to incorporate elements of an uncertainty-agency model.

- Second, we need to develop pastoral transition training for resigning pastors, lay leaders, and congregations. If agency is indeed an important antidote to uncertainty, people need to understand how they can play their appropriate role.

- Third, we need to develop the tools and training to support an evidence-based approach to pastoral transitions that customizes to context. Transparency is critical to empowering people.

- Fourth, we need to expand our research effort relative to pastoral transitions. One way to do this is by developing a central database that aggregates assessment results from churches in transition.

- Fifth, we need to identify patterns from the research that will improve the predictability of decision-making including failure paths and best practices.

- Sixth, we need to train regional association leaders who support churches during pastoral transitions in utilizing an uncertainty-agency model.

- Seventh, we need to develop resources, including preaching clinics that will strengthen the transition preaching of interim pastors.

- Eighth, we need to provide interim pastors with evidence-based flexibility training.

- Ninth, we need to develop a biblical-theological rationale for an uncertainty-agency approach that focuses on mission, stewardship, giftedness, and empowerment.

LIMITATIONS OF THIS STUDY

This study was conducted by investigating aggregated data from churches at different points along a pastoral transition trajectory. Self-selection errors could result in nonrepresentative samples from these various groups. We believe that these errors are minimized by the nearly universal use of interim pastors for churches in transition. This is less likely in larger churches that are experimenting with different succession approaches, including succession planning. It also is less likely in churches that are too small to call an interim pastor. Ideally, a research project would engage individual churches in a longitudinal process of assessment at five points: pre-transition, transition entry, interim midterm, pastor start-up, and two-year trending. How to secure a commitment to such a research project is left to future minds.

About the Author

JRussell Crabtree is an Ohio native and graduate of Ohio State University with a degree in engineering physics. He worked in research at the Eastman Kodak Company for three years in the area of optics and electrostatic control systems. He left industry to attend seminary and served as a pastor for twenty years. In 1998, Russ founded and served for five years as the executive director of Montaña de Luz, a project providing hospice care for abandoned children with HIV-AIDS in Honduras. In the wake of Hurricane Mitch he founded and directed Ohio Hurricane Relief for Central America. He was the cofounder and president of Holy Cow! Consulting, which provides strategic planning, training, and organizational assessment. He also founded and currently directs BestMinds, a company specializing in awareness and intervention training for suicide and domestic violence. He has worked with cross-professional teams in counties with high suicide rates to develop prevention and intervention strategies; he helped shape the suicide prevention plan developed by the state of Ohio.

Russ has extensive experience in assisting organizations across the United States with strategic planning, mediation, customer surveys, and training. He has worked with many different kinds of organizations including churches, libraries, colleges, and an arboretum. He has developed training for organizations in strategic planning, conflict management, team building, staff morale, customer service, and enhancing board function.

As a former Presbyterian pastor, Russ served in small, midsize, and large churches in New York and Ohio. In that role, he was active in his regional association (presbytery) and worked in the areas of strategic planning, energy conservation, human sexuality, church consultation, presbytery staffing, and administrative oversight. He has served as a consultant to every level of the church in areas such as succession planning, strategic planning, and organizational assessment.

He has developed congregational and regional association assessment tools and has maintained a substantial database on church characteristics and congregations of all sizes and contexts. He is the creator of *Portal*, an assessment instrument for regional associations, *Pulse*, a staff climate assessment tool for larger churches and regional associations, and *FocalPoints*, an assessment tool for boards and leadership teams. He has developed a number of products for churches in transition.

Russ coauthored a book with Carolyn Weese that was published in August 2004 entitled *The Elephant in the Board Room: Developing a Pastoral Succession Plan for Your Church*. The concepts of this book have been incorporated in a workbook developed to assist church leaders in pastoral succession planning. Using these materials, he has assisted some of the largest churches in the United States in developing succession plans. In 2008, he published *The Fly in the Ointment: Why Denominations Aren't Helping Their Churches and How They Can*. In 2012, he published *Owl Sight: Evidence-Based Discernment and the Promise of Organizational Intelligence for Ministry*. Other works include *Mountain of Light; The Story of Montana de Luz*, published in April 2005; and *A Second Day*, which was republished in April 2014.

Russ lives with his wife, Shawn, in Asheville, North Carolina. Together, they have six children and twelve grandchildren.

For further information contact:

J. Russell Crabtree
BestMinds, LLC
614-208-4090
fe@aseconddays.com